THE NEXT NORMAL

BY PETER J. PITTS

COGNITO PRESS

First Printing: 2022

ISBN 978-1-716-03997-3

Cognito Press

757 Third Avenue
New York, NY 10017

www.cmpi.org

Graphic design by Mandi Vollmer.

"He who wrestles with us strengthens our nerves and sharpens our skill. Our antagonist is our helper." EDMOND BURKE

AUTHOR'S NOTE

This book is dedicated to all the healthcare professionals, first responders and frontline workers who put their lives at risk for all of us. Banging pots wasn't enough, but it was a start.

To Sweet Jane, "For better or for worse."

To the women and men of the FDA and the biopharmaceutical industry who pulled off a miracle bringing diagnostics, therapeutics and vaccines to market at warp speed, helping issue in a new era of cooperation within and between the broader healthcare ecosystem. It's amazing what we can accomplish when we work together for the common good.

And to the courageous staff of 54 Riverside Drive who, in the teeth of the pandemic, hunkered down, masked-up and braved the highways, byways, subways, sidewalks, roads and tunnels of New York City, coming to work every day. They have my deepest respect and are forever part of our family.

Peter J. Pitts
New York City
January 2022

CONTENTS

CHAPTER FIVE: SCIENCE IS BACK

INTRODUCTION: "SCIENCE PERFECTS GENIUS AND MODERATES THAT FURY OF THE FANCY THAT CANNOT CONTAIN ITSELF WITHIN THE BOUNDS OF REASON."

CHAPTER SIX: THE LESSONS OF COVID-19

INTRODUCTION: "WE CAN DRAW LESSONS FROM THE PAST, BUT WE CANNOT LIVE IN IT."

CHAPTER SEVEN: SPEAKING TO/THROUGH AMERICA'S NEWSPAPER OF RECORD

INTRODUCTION: "PLEASE GIVE ME SOME GOOD ADVICE IN YOUR NEXT LETTER. I PROMISE NOT TO FOLLOW IT."

INTRODUCTION

"Human history becomes more and more a race between education and catastrophe."

H.G. WELLS

Why "The Next Normal"? Over the course of the COVID-19 pandemic, during dozens of media interviews, virtual conferences, and Zoom encounters, people asked me what the "new" normal will look like. I fundamentally disagree with the premise of this question because, when it comes to healthcare, there will never be a "new" normal. Healthcare will always be in a constant state of change — and that's a good thing. What will always be just around the corner is *the Next Normal*. Stasis isn't always good, especially if you believe in the power of innovation. But the status quo is a harsh mistress. If we have learned nothing else from COVID-19 we should remember and embrace the warning of management guru W. Edwards Deming, who said, "It is not necessary to change. Survival is not mandatory."

CHAPTER ONE
Value Equity

"You cannot escape the responsibility of tomorrow by evading it today."

ABRAHAM LINCOLN

"Equity" and "equality" are not synonyms. When it comes to healthcare, "equity" means similar outcomes across race, gender, socioeconomic conditions, and political borders. One of the key lessons from the COVID-19 experience is that we're all in this together. We rise or fall together, and "redlining" healthcare (purposefully, through ignorance or lassitude) is an evil that lurks throughout the healthcare ecosystem. There are many strategies and tactics to consider. And at the top of the list is a reconsideration and renaissance of personal responsibility.

Health Literacy: The Common Denominator of Healthcare Progress

By Peter J. Pitts and Emily Freeman

Originally published in *The Patient*, July 7, 2021

Introduction: Embracing the Lessons of COVID-19

Perhaps the most important lesson learned from the COVID-19 experience is that American health illiteracy kills. From confusion over the value of wearing protective masks and social distancing (How are viruses transmitted?) to vaccine skepticism (How do vaccines work?), from confusion over the value of hydroxychloroquine (How are data collected and what do they mean?) to doubts about the safety and efficacy of products available through Emergency Use Authorizations (How does the US Food and Drug Administration review process work?), the dearth of health literacy has not only slowed down the US response against COVID-19, it has placed thorny societal problems along the path to victory over the virus. Nature abhors a vacuum — and so does social media.

Health literacy comprises two parts:[2]

Personal health literacy is the degree to which individuals have the ability to find, understand, and use information and services to inform health-related decisions and actions for themselves and others.

Organizational health literacy is the degree to which organizations equitably enable individuals to find, understand, and use information and services to inform health-related decisions and actions for themselves and others.

As we study our national responses to COVID-19 to better plan for the next public health emergency, a key global learning is that health literacy is an integral part of pandemic preparedness and a broader facilitator of positive healthcare behavior and outcomes. Health literacy facilitates public health messages that are not only understandable but motivational and actionable.

According to the US Health Resources and Services Administration, health literacy is "the degree to which individuals have the capacity to obtain, process and understand basic health information and services needed to make appropriate health decisions".[3] Health literacy is capacity building. It is crucial infrastructure development. And it is being ignored.

The Value of Health Literacy

The value of health literacy extends far beyond the boundaries of COVID-19. Education leads to fact-based empowerment and an educated healthcare consumer can be a potent change agent.

Consider medication adherence and compliance. Medication nonadherence is widespread with nonadherence rates that range from 25 to 50 percent.[4] Every year, 125,000 Americans die from not taking their medications, a staggering number that also costs the US health system some $289 billion annually.[5] One potent tool for recapturing and redirecting these healthcare resources is health literacy. Safe and effective. Knowledge is power.

Low levels of health literacy are a source of health disparities among disadvantaged communities and minorities. Of the nearly 77 million Americans who struggle with health-related reading tasks, 65 percent are minorities.[6] The issue of health literacy and minority communities is not new, but it has been rediscovered because of COVID-19, specifically because of the problem of vaccine hesitancy driven by historic distrust of government-sponsored healthcare programs[7] and a perceived lack of clinical trial diversity.

One reason minorities and communities of color have been hesitant to embrace COVID-19 vaccines is that they do not see "people like me" in clinical trials.[8] An easy excuse is that groups are represented proportionally to their ranking in the general population. But that is an excuse. As with many health conditions (e.g., diabetes mellitus, cardiovascular disease, cancer), "diverse" communities suffer disproportionally. COVID-19 is only the most recent example with death rates and serious manifestations of the virus far outpacing the relative impact on White America. African-American individuals are experiencing COVID-19 death tolls exceeding 1 in 800 nationally, while White Americans are experiencing a death toll at 1 in 3,125 nationally. African-American individuals have COVID-19 death rates of more than 2.7 times those of White Americans.[9] There are many reasons for this and there is no single "magic bullet" solution. Health literacy, alone and in combination with other "therapies," however, should be considered at or near the top of the list of post-pandemic public health priorities.

Health Literacy as a Tool in Achieving Clinical Trial Diversity
In an age of precision medicine,[10] health literacy can be a powerful tool to improve both clinical trial diversity and overall data sensitivity. Addressing diversity in clinical trials is a bellwether issue when it comes to advancing health literacy. We are all learning the nuanced differences between "equality" and "equity." Equality means each individual or group of people is given the same resources or opportunities. Equity recognizes that each person has different circumstances and allocates the exact resources and opportunities needed to reach an equal outcome.[11]

A recent study of Pfizer-sponsored clinical trials[12] showed that between 2011 and 2020, Black or African-American participants made up 14.3 percent of

212 trials for which data on race were collected. African-American individuals represent about 13.4 percent of the US population. But when broken down by trial, only about half of Pfizer's studies (56.1 percent) surpassed census levels for Black participants. Only 15.8 percent of Pfizer's oncology trials reached census levels for Black participants, compared with 78.9 percent for White participants. The percentage of trials overall to exceed census levels for White participants was 51.4 percent.

Asian-American individuals made up 3.1 percent of trials compared with 5.9 percent of the US population. Hispanic or Latinx participants represented 15.9 percent of trials, vs. 18.5 percent of the population. In total, 16 percent of Pfizer's trials surpassed census levels for Asian participants, compared with 14.2 percent for Native Hawaiian or Pacific Islanders, and just 8.5 percent for American Indian or Alaskan Native individuals.

Those numbers are par for the course in biopharma, where minority groups have historically been left out of clinical trials. Of the 53 drugs approved this past year, Black patients represented about 8 percent of participants in the trials that regulators based their decisions on (and for which data on race were collected).[13]

Why are there not more minorities and people of color recruited for clinical trials in the US? The usual and customary explanation is because of historic distrust of the government (e.g., Tuskegee, Henrietta Lacks).[14] But this is only one of many issues. Participation in clinical trials research is a rigorous and demanding enterprise. Another associated long-term impediment is that physicians and other research professionals have their own cognitive biases concerning who they believe will comply with difficult therapeutic regimens[15] required for proper participation in clinical trials. Many physicians believe African-American individuals are two-thirds as likely to be adherent as are their White patients.[15]

We must be aware of and fight against such normative bias (aka "racism"). Despite these factors, research demonstrates that minorities are, in fact, willing to participate in clinical trials. Minority groups are as willing to participate as White American individuals but are not asked to (literally) sit down and roll up their sleeves.[16] In a health literacy issue brief, the Secretary's Advisory Committee noted, "As health literacy research and practice have accumulated, we now more fully understand that responsibility for health literacy extends beyond individuals to include the organizations and professionals who create and deliver health information and services."[17] Physicians and healthcare professionals must also advance their own health literacy. Perhaps we need continuing medical education for health literacy.

Health Literacy and Pharmacovigilance

Pharmacovigilance traditionally relies on physicians and pharmaceutical manufacturers as the two main pillars of reporting, with the overwhelming volume coming from industry (as well as a small but growing and significant contribution coming directly from patients and healthcare providers).[18] Pharmacovigilance has not been a large experimental ground for patient participation; on the one hand, this is because it has always been perceived as an area where only healthcare professionals have the right competence to deal with adverse events and the associated risks, and on the other hand, because patients have not historically been encouraged to play an active role in this issue. With an increasing number of drugs being approved on shorter trials that involve fewer patients, obtaining timely and accurate reports of adverse events and side effects after approval from all members of the post-marketing ecosystem is more important than ever.[19]

In both the US and the European Union, proactive pharmacovigilance efforts by both regulators and pharmaceutical companies have escalated in recent times through (among other efforts) an increased use of real-world data, gathered and validated across multiple sources after a medicine has been approved.[20] A more health literate population can make post-marketing surveillance a more complete three-dimensional proposition.

The value of obtaining the patient perspective regarding the benefit–risk profile of medicinal products is being increasingly acknowledged by regulatory authorities.[21] Enhanced health literacy has the very real potential to enable a more significant contribution from a broader constituency of patients and caregivers of timely and accurate knowledge on issues that arise in the post-marketing environment including adverse event reporting, quality-of-life information,[22] and the collection of real-world data.[23] Health literacy is a potent tool to advance 21st-century pharmacovigilance.

The Need for a National "Health Literacy Czar"

Health literacy programs will not spring fully developed and ready for action from the head of Zeus, Anthony Fauci (the director of the US National Institute of Allergy and Infectious Diseases) or anyone else. Another lesson learned from the COVID-19 experience is that, when it comes to healthcare communications, one size does not fit all, but that the federal government can play the role of Convener-in-Chief. Content, curriculum, funding, logistics, measurement, and other details must be a consensus-driven proposition. And it must be politics-free. Step one is to agree on what "success" looks like. Nobody said it was going to be easy.

We suggest the US president appoint a "Health Literacy Czar," empowered (initially) to develop a long-term national strategy aimed at increasing the levels of knowledge on a wide range of topics across a broad national constituency. Such a plan could include a national K-12 educational curriculum for students, more advanced modules for medical and pharmacy schools, and professional and post-graduate professional education courses (e.g., continuing medical education). America's Health Literacy Czar. A good first step would be to establish a Presidential Blue-Ribbon Commission on Advancing America Health Literacy in the 21st Century.

The Urgency of Personal Responsibility

To advance an honest and robust health literacy agenda, we must understand and embrace another key learning from the COVID-19 experience — that when we all work together (e.g., government, academia, industry, healthcare providers, caregivers, educators, community leaders, patients) we can achieve miraculous things at warp speed. Seneca said, "Life speeds on with a hurried step." When it comes to a bold long-term national program to achieve a high national health literacy standard, the three key facilitators of success are trust, transparency, and broad participation.

Conclusions

Health literacy is not passive, it is participatory and a foundation for positive behavioral change. Individuals with adequate levels of health literacy have the ability to take responsibility for their own health as well as family and community well-being.[24] The Office of Behavioral and Social Sciences Research was created by Congress in 1993 and is responsible for coordinating the health-relevant behavioral and social sciences and identifying challenges and opportunities to advance these sciences at the National Institutes of Science.[25] Increasing its funding should be a top post-pandemic priority. Just as there is no "magic pill" for good health, there is no "magic solution" for health literacy. It will take time, hard work, and commitment to convene the critical disciplines that can inform programs, practices, and metrics. There will be mistakes, setbacks, and frustration. Most importantly, success rests on personal responsibility.

REFERENCES

1. Coles quotables, quotation #5265. Available from: http://www.quotationspage.com/search.php?homesearch=literacy&startsearch=Search. Accessed 11 June 2021.

2. History of health literacy definitions. 2020. Available from: https://health.gov/our-work/healthy-people/healthy-people-2030/health-literacy-healthy-people-2030/history-health-literacy-definitions. Accessed 11 June 2021.

3. Health Resources and Services Administration. 2019. Available from: https://www.hrsa.gov/about/organization/bureaus/ohe/health-literacy/index.html. Accessed 11 June 2021.

4. Iuga AO, McGuire MJ. Adherence and healthcare costs. Risk Manag Healthc Policy. 2014;7:35–44. Available from: https://www.ncbi.nlm.nih.gov/pmc/articles/PMC3934668/. Accessed 11 June 2021.

5. Cut prices to boost medication adherence. 2019. Available from: https://www.healtheconomics.com/industry-news/opinion-cut-prices-to-boost-medication-adherence. Accessed 11 June 2021.

6. Why health literacy is important for diverse communities. 2018. Available from: https://www.ahip.org/why-health-literacy-is-important-for-diverse-communities/. Accessed 11 June 2021.

7. Laurencin CT. Addressing justified vaccine hesitancy in the black community. J Racial Ethn Health Disparities. 2021;8(3):543–6. https://doi.org/10.1007/s40615-021-01025-4.

8. Driving equity in clinical trials with a diversity-first mindset. 2021. Available from: https://www.linkedin.com/pulse/driving-equity-clinical-trials-diversity-first-viraj-narayanan/. Accessed 11 June 2021.

9. The color of coronavirus: COVID-19 deaths by race and ethnicity in the US. 2021. Available from: https://www.apmresearchlab.org/covid/deaths-by-race. Accessed 11 June 2021.

10. Precision medicine. 2021. Available from: https://en.wikipedia.org/wiki/Precision_medicine. Accessed 11 June 2021.

11. Equity vs. equality: what's the difference? 2020. Available from: https://onlinepublichealth.gwu.edu/resources/equity-vs-equality/. Accessed 11 June 2021.

12. Rottas M, Thadeio P, Simons R et al. Demographic diversity of participants in Pfizer sponsored clinical trials in the United States. Contemporary Clinical trials 2021; 2021. https://doi.org/10.1016/j.cct.2021.106421. Accessed 11 June 2021.

13. Pfizer publishes clinical trial diversity data from past decade, showing there's much work to be done. 2021. Available from: https://endpts.com/pfizer-publishes-clinical-trial-diversity-data-from-past-decade-showing-theres-much-work-to-be-done. Accessed 11 June 2021.

14. Scharff DP, Mathews KJ, Jackson P et al. More than Tuskegee: understanding mistrust about research participation. J Health Care Poor Underserved. 2010;21(3):879–97. https://www.ncbi.nlm.nih.gov/pmc/articles/PMC4354806/. Accessed 11 June 2021

15. van Ryn M, Burke J. The effect of patient race and socio-economic status on physicians' perceptions of patients. Soc Sci Med 2000;50(6):813–28. https://doi.org/10.1016/s0277-9536(99)00338-x. Accessed 11 June 2021.

16. Wendler D, Kington R, Madans J et al. Are racial and ethnic minorities less willing to participate in health research? Plos Med. 2006;3(2):e19. https://doi.org/10.1371/journal.pmed.0030019.6.

17. Office of Disease Prevention and Health Promotion. 2020. Available from: https://health.gov/our-work/healthy-people/healthy-people-2030/health-literacy-healthy-people-2030/history-health-literacy-definitions. Accessed 11 June 2021.

18. Pitts PJ, Le Louet H, Moride Y et al. 21st century pharmacovigilance: efforts, roles, and responsibilities. Lancet Oncol. 2016;17(11):e486–92. https://doi.org/10.1016/S1470-2045(16)30312-6.

19. Paola K, Claudio G. The value of direct patient reporting in pharmacovigilance. Ther Adv Drug Safety. 2020. https://doi.org/10.1177/2042098620940164.

20. Pitts PJ, Le Louet H. Advancing drug safety through prospective pharmacovigilance. Ther Innov Regul Sci. 2018;52(4):400–402. https://doi.org/10.1177/2168479018766887.

21. Smith MY, Benattia I. The patient's voice in pharmacovigilance: pragmatic approaches to building a patient-centric drug safety organization. Drug Saf. 2016;39(9):779–85. https://doi.org/10.1177/2168479018766887.

22. Morris J, Perez D, McNoe B. The use of quality of life data in clinical practice. Qual Life Res. 1998;7(1):85–91. https://doi.org/10.1023/a:1008893007068.

23. Real-world data (RWD) and real-world evidence (RWE) are playing an increasing role in health care decisions. 2020. Available from: https://www.fda.gov/science-research/science-and-research-special-topics/real-world-evidence. Accessed 11 June 2021.

24. McQueen D, Kickbusch I, Potvin L, Pelikan JM, Balbo L, Abel T, editors. Health and modernity. The role of theory in health promotion. Springer; 2007.

25. National Institutes of Health Office of Behavioral and Social Sciences Research. 2021. Available from: https://obssr.od.nih.gov/about/. Accessed 11 June 2021.

Comment on "Health Literacy: The Common Denominator of Healthcare Progress"

By Halah Ibrahim and Satish Chandrasekhar Nair
Originally published in *The Patient*, October 18, 2021

Dear Editor,

We read with great interest the commentary "Health Literacy: The Common Denominator of Healthcare Progress" by Pitts and Freeman in the September 2021 issue of *The Patient*.[1] We applaud the authors for highlighting the important, but often ignored, impact of health literacy on health outcomes. The World Health Organization considers health literacy to be one of the most important health indicators.[2] There is a large and growing body of literature documenting the adverse consequences of inadequate health literacy, including decreased screening and preventive services and decreased compliance with treatments.[3] This results in increased use of emergency services, increased hospitalizations and, ultimately, higher mortality rates.[3] Despite its importance, health literacy is a global public health concern. International data confirm that many countries struggle with inadequate health literacy rates.[4] The European Health Literacy survey noted limited health literacy in 47 percent of respondents, inadequate health literacy in 12 percent, and an additional 35 percent with problematic health literacy.[5] In the United Arab Emirates, we found that over 60 percent of the population surveyed possessed inadequate health literacy.[6] A nationwide study in the United States revealed that 36 percent of Americans had basic and below basic health literacy rates.[7]

The COVID-19 pandemic has focused attention on the intersection between government regulations, social policy and health outcomes. As the authors state, the disproportionately high morbidity and mortality of COVID-19 on communities of color is multi-factorial, and includes disinformation campaigns that targeted Black and Latinx patients, historical mistrust in government institutions, and the systemic racism that has long existed in research and healthcare, but only recently entered the public conversation on health disparities.[8] The authors suggest that health literacy should be an integral part of pandemic preparedness. In fact, as pandemic-imposed changes to the healthcare system become permanent, such as telehealth services, health inequities may continue to increase for those unable to access or use advanced technology.[8]

We agree with the authors that improving health literacy should be a national priority. Programs to improve health literacy can lead to improved patient and population health outcomes. The concept of appointing a "health literacy czar" for the United States is interesting. The fear is that with the current politicization of all government agencies and roles, it may be difficult for an individual to bring forth meaningful change. A longitudinal and multi-pronged government approach is necessary, including tackling disparities in the nation's education system. Research on health inequities has consistently shown a correlation between low health literacy, decreased educational attainment and poor health outcomes.[9] In this regard, strategies to improve health literacy may, in turn, improve health outcomes in patients with lower levels of education.

While government-led approaches are necessary, the healthcare community has an important role in tackling health literacy. Targeted interventions are necessary to prevent the marginalization of all patient populations, including racial and ethnic minorities, elderly patients, and those with chronic medical conditions, to ensure that they fully understand and are engaged with all healthcare decisions. In addition to ongoing efforts to recognize and address implicit and explicit bias in research and healthcare, individual healthcare professionals and hospitals can prioritize health literacy in daily interactions. First, healthcare providers and researchers should assess every patient's ability to understand and process the information that they are provided. This becomes especially difficult with virtual technology, where facial and body cues may not be as evident. As such, allocating appropriate time for patient visits and ensuring that all questions are answered becomes increasingly important. Integrating multilingual staff into the clinical teams, including case coordinators and patient representatives, can help overcome some language barriers. Hospitals can also design and implement professional development programs that focus specifically on using universal health literacy precautions during patient-provider interactions. Tips include avoiding medical terminology, explaining information in small, easily understandable pieces, and assessing comprehension. Using pictures and visual aids can also improve patient understanding.[10] As Pitts and Freeman state, there is no "magic solution" for health literacy. It will, indeed, take "time, hard work, and commitment to convene the critical disciplines that can inform programs, practices, and metrics." As healthcare professionals, we can each do our part.

REFERENCES

1. Pitts PJ, Freeman E. Health literacy: the common denominator of healthcare progress. Patient. 2021;14(5):455–8.

2. World Health Organization. World Health Statistics. https://www.who.int/gho/publications/world_health_statistics/EN_WHS2015_Part2.pdf?ua=1. Accessed 16 Sept 2021.

3. Berkman ND, Sheridan SL, Donahue KE, Halpern DJ, Crotty K. Low health literacy and health outcomes: an updated systematic review. Ann Intern Med. 2011;155(2):97–107.

4. Nair SC, Satish KP, Sreedharan J, Ibrahim H. Assessing health literacy in the eastern and middle-eastern cultures. BMC Public Health. 2016;16:831.

5. Sørensen K, van den Broucke S, Fullam J, Doyle G, Pelikan J, Slonska Z, et al. Health literacy and public health: a systematic review and integration of definitions and models. BMC Public Health. 2012;12:80.

6. Nair SC, Satish KP, Sreedharan J, Muttappallymyalil J, Ibrahim H. Improving health literacy critical to optimize telemedicine, the future of global healthcare. Telemed E-Health. 2020;26(11):1325.

7. The Health Literacy of America's Adults. https://nces.ed.gov/pubs2006/2006483.pdf. Accessed 16 Sept 2021.

8. Scharff DP, Mathews KJ, Jackson P, et al. More than Tuskegee: understanding mistrust about research participation. J Health Care Poor Underserved. 2010;21(3):879–97.

9. van der Heide I, Rademakers J, Schipper M, Droomers M, Sørensen K, Uiters E. Health literacy of Dutch adults: a cross sectional survey. BMC Public Health. 2013;13:179.

10. Hersh L, Salzman B, Snyderman D. Health literacy in primary care practice. Am Fam Physician. 2015;92(2):118–24.

Authors' Reply to Ibrahim and Nair's Comment on: "Health Literacy: The Common Denominator of Healthcare Progress"

By Peter J. Pitts and Emily Freeman

Originally published in *The Patient*, October 18, 2021

Dear Editor-in-Chief,

We thank Ibrahim and Nair[1] for their thoughtful comments on our paper, "Health Literacy: The Common Denominator of Healthcare Progress."[2] They affirm that health literacy is not just a Western phenomenon. (Over 60 percent of the population surveyed in the United Arab Emirates possessed inadequate health literacy.[3]) Health literacy afflicts people of all races, nationalities, and socioeconomic conditions. However, unlike a vaccine that can be safe and effective across borders and other divides, there is no inoculation that can eradicate the problems associated with low rates of health literacy. While there are likely common techniques that could be considered "best practices" (the involvement of local healthcare providers and other trusted local voices, a common lexicography),[4] every nation and community of nations (such as the United Arab Emirates, the broader Gulf region, the Levant, the Mashriq, and the Maghreb) will have to consider and design programs specifically suited to their own populations and unique domestic circumstances. A unique "Arab" health literacy strategy will not be unique enough. Granularity is essential. We must also recognize that in nations such as India, it will be impossible to address health literacy without also addressing literacy. (As per the 2021 census, the literacy rate of India is 74.04 percent[5] and 90 percent of the people in India have low health literacy.[6]) But the most important problem for every nation (after, of course, recognition of the problem) is resources. Speeches at conferences by astute and dedicated thought leaders, peer-reviewed papers in prestigious journals, and enhanced academic curricula for healthcare professionals are a good start, but without appropriate financial and human resources (on a continuing basis), any efforts to successfully advance health literacy will fail. As we have learned from the COVID-19 experience, developing the tools to combat the virus are for naught if we do not recognize the logistical, societal, and financial barriers to success.

REFERENCES

1. Ibrahim H, Nair SC. Comment on "health literacy: the common denominator of healthcare progress." Patient. 2021. https://doi.org/10.1007/s40271-021-00556-6.

2. Pitts PJ, Freeman E. Health literacy: the common denominator of healthcare progress. Patient. 2021;14(5):455–8.

3. Nair SC, Satish KP, Sreedharan J, Muttappallymyalil J, Ibrahim H. Improving health literacy critical to optimize telemedicine, the future of global healthcare. Telemed J E Health. 2020;26(11):1325.

4. Mackert M, Ball J, Lopez N, et al. Health literacy awareness training for healthcare workers: improving knowledge and intentions to use clear communication techniques. Patient Educ Couns. 2011;85(3):e225–8.

5. IndiaCensus.net. https://www.indiacensus.net/literacy-rate.php. Accessed 8 Oct 2021.

6. Kumar R. Health literacy a must to empower patients. https://www.tribuneindia.com/news/archive/comment/health-literacy-a-must-to-empower-patients-752945. Accessed 8 Oct 2021.

A 21st-Century Lexicon of Value

By Peter J. Pitts

Originally published in *Morning Consult*, January 7, 2019

What is value-based healthcare? Why is it so important? And why is it so difficult to measure?

In a world of increasingly complex innovation and finite financial resources, these three questions are crucial to advancing 21st-century healthcare technology assessment. Such inquiries are devilishly contentious and complicated. In order to answer them, academics, government officials, practitioners and patients must agree on, among other things, a pallet of harmonized terminology: a lexicon of value.

We stand at a value-based inflection point. Public and private health systems and their constituent and overlapping stakeholders are being held increasingly accountable for the value their decisions, products and services provide to individual patients and society at large, yet the emergence of value-based healthcare is consistently hindered by a lack of transparent and standardized outcome data.

The general consensus is that healthcare ought to be driven by a relentless focus on delivering outcomes that truly matter to patients. How can problems be addressed and questions answered so that opportunities can be realized?

Value in healthcare is not a vague or theoretical concept. It is defined by a simple equation: outcomes/costs. Patient outcomes designate the end results of healthcare expressed in terms of quality of life and functional scores based on validated methodologies.

Over the years, health economists have developed sophisticated tools and techniques to measure the denominator — costs. However, the numerator — patient outcomes — remains ill defined and unevenly measured even though it reflects the true meaning of "success."

The concept of measuring the actual therapeutic outcomes of treatment was first proposed over a century ago by Dr. Ernest Amory Codman, known for his advocacy of the "End Result Idea." The "idea" was simply the premise that hospital staffs would follow every patient they treat long enough to determine whether or not the treatment was successful, then learn from any failures and how to avoid those situations in the future. In 1914, Massachusetts General Hospital refused Codman's plan for evaluating surgeon competence, and he lost his staffing privileges.

Transparency of patient outcomes data has become a nascent but powerful tool for health authorities to compare providers head-to-head, driving competition and advancing quality in a race to the top.

The US Department of Health and Human Services has created an online portal that discloses, per hospital, indicators such as readmissions rates, complications and mortality, payment and value of care. HHS Secretary Alex Azar recently announced the inpatient prospective payment system rule, which contains proposals to advance a healthcare system that pays for value, as well as a request for information regarding future value-based reforms. Per Azar, this rule is designed to "disrupt our existing system and deliver real value for healthcare consumers. ... We are going to move toward a system that provides better care for Americans at a lower cost."

Every subject "under the light" changes its behavior. This mimetic reaction is hardwired human behavior and applies to policymakers, practitioners, providers and patients alike.

Nobody wants to lag behind, and pride is a powerful catalyst for team building and individual improvement. Transparency enables and encourages self-evaluation, which is a nonpaternalistic way to align best practices (political, medical, etc.) that deliver higher outcomes.

Measuring patient-reported outcome measures (PROMs) requires complex case mix adjustments. It is much easier to measure traditional items such as volume of care, average length of stay, compliance to administrative procedures — and ignore patient outcomes. With the myriad of unvalidated proxy indicators that health systems use to define quality, we are losing the ability to accurately define "success."

For example, patient-reported experience measurements (PREMs) assess a patient's satisfaction during hospitalization. Indicators often measure the quality of food, cleanliness of the room, the procedures for the discharge, communication with the medical team and various waiting times during hospitalization.

Are higher PREM scores valid predictors of better PROMs? While there is certainly a link between hospitalization and hospitality, hospitals are not hotels. While a guest may choose to return to a good hotel, a good hospital is largely predicated on not having to come back. PREMs measure outputs that matter to hospital administrators. PROMs measure healthcare outcomes that matter to patients and healthcare providers. Not surprisingly, patient response rates to PREM surveys are on average less than 20 percent compared to 90 percent for PROM questionnaires.

The goal of value-based healthcare is to facilitate making "outcomes" the defining variable in the multifaceted decision-making process, superseding both cost and "quality." In that respect, VBHC becomes "21st-century tendering" for both payers and patients. VBHC plus quality becomes "3D quality." It advances the concept of quality from a "soft" to a "hard" measurement tool.

PROM registries are complex to set up but represent a transformative investment that will change medical behaviors, enable patients to orient themselves to both the most appropriate practitioner and sites of care and generate savings for public and private payers. Providers who disclose their outcomes will be preferred by patients and payers. Those who do not subscribe to outcome-based measurements will be viewed with suspicion or derision — or both.

The future is becoming increasingly clear. Value-based healthcare turns concepts such as "value and quality" into "hard data." It is time to adopt the same language to measure success in healthcare with indicators that truly matter to patients. Value-based healthcare isn't about harmonization of decision-making; it's about harmonization of design and process. This is crucial as other HTA "harmonization" efforts are heralding themselves as a quasi-nice "one-size-fits-all" approach. "Value" should be a constant, and political entities should make decisions based on constants — but decisions can be different based on different national needs, priorities, and biases.

Value over Volume: Maximizing Resources by Prioritizing Value: The Dubai Healthcare Experience

By Mohammad Naser Fargaly, Sara Al Dallal, and Peter J. Pitts

Originally published in the *Journal of Commercial Biotechnology*, December 2021

Introduction

Dubai is often known as the "home of superlatives:" the biggest malls, the tallest building, the newest technologies. But the most important (and often unrecognized) local trait is speed to best practice implementation. In more Western parlance, the emirate isn't just about indoor skiing in searing summer heat. It's public policy action. Consider Dubai's healthcare delivery system. The emirate talks the talk and walks the walk. Mandatory health insurance was enacted in 2014 requiring that by 2016 every employee and dependent residing in Dubai must be medically insured.[1] Four years later, close to 100 percent of Dubai's population is now covered and have financial access to healthcare. (See Figure 1.) And it's not just about a speed trophy — the results are also impressive.

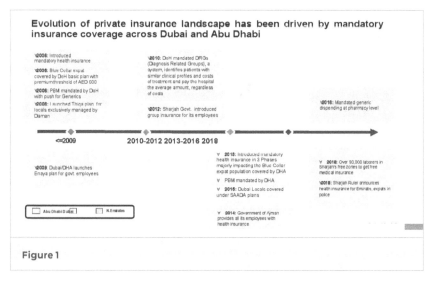

Figure 1

The mission of the Dubai Health Authority is to transform healthcare delivery by fostering innovative and integrated care models and enhancing community engagement. The Authority's three goals (see Figure 2) are designed to move the emirate's healthcare system forward by being mutually supportive, constituency inclusive, accountable and outcomes-based.

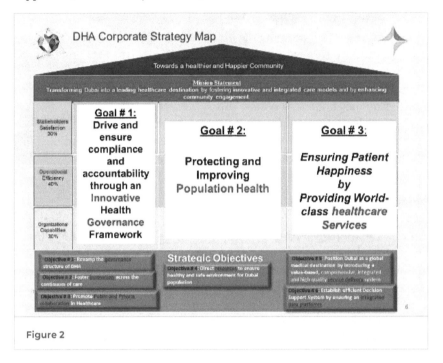

Figure 2

The Authority strives to reach these goals through six core values:

1. Customer centricity
2. Efficiency
3. Engaged and motivated workforce
4. Accountability and transparency
5. Innovation
6. Excellence

Dubai's healthcare policy leadership has adopted a strategy to drive and ensure compliance and accountability through an innovative health governance framework. At its core, Dubai's healthcare strategy begins with its Care Model Innovation Program. This key initiative is designed to promote innovation and efficiency and ensure that Dubai residents (citizens) and visitors (noncitizen residents) have access to high-quality services across the continuum of care.

The strategy introduces innovative care models to fill existing care delivery gaps and enable an integrated cost-effective, patient- and innovation-oriented care delivery system.

Dubai's Care Model Innovation design contains 10 distinct aspects:

1. Develop and implement a strategy for special-needs patients.
2. Innovate in the delivery of ambulatory surgery.
3. Introduce and promote the use of telemedicine solutions.
4. Introduce innovative medical technologies in the provision of healthcare services.
5. Promote innovation culture.
6. Enhance home and remote care.
7. Reinforce the use of patient engagement tools.
8. Develop pharma interventions to provide solutions beyond the pill.
9. Innovate in the delivery of rehabilitation care.
10. Continuously innovate the healthcare delivery ecosystem.

Value over Volume

At DUPHAT 2021 (the largest pharmaceutical event in Middle East and Africa),[2] Dr. Mohamed Farghaly (head of the Dubai Health Authority's insurance medical regulation department) outlined both the strategic implications and tactical realities of pharmaceutical costs on Dubai's health insurance system. The key "red thread" of his presentation was "value over volume" — that cost, while receiving the lion's share of healthcare headlines, is only one of many above-the-line variables with value (defined as positive patient outcomes) the driving "bottom line" denominator of the healthcare equation. (See Figure 3.)

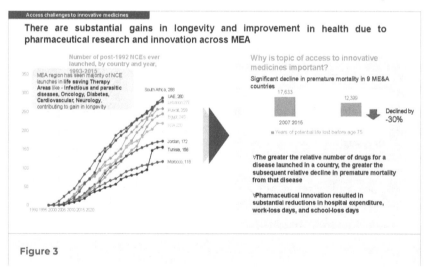

Figure 3

Dr. Farghaly began his presentation by making clear what volume-based cost-containment options were off the table: Brand-to-generic substitution at point of dispensation (pharmacies) and nonmedical switching from brand to generic drugs or innovator biologics to biosimilars, mandatory step therapy, or in any way interfering with a physician's authority to practice medicine as she sees fit for any given patient. According to Dr. Farghaly, empowered physicians deliver better results and, hence, greater value to both their patients and the healthcare system in Dubai.

In a recent study of German cardiologists,[3] researchers found that more than 14 percent of physicians in the quantitative study and over one-third of physicians in the qualitative study chose not to participate in a government-initiated cardiology program because of concerns related to freedom — especially out of fear for their own professional autonomy as such or in relation to prescription regulations as well as the patients' free choice of medical practitioners. As one physician commented, "I think professional autonomy is heavily threatened here by the cardiology program." They especially perceived an emergence of unilateral dependence instead of cooperation. This is likely based on the imbalance of power within the program.

Research from other national programs reinforce the concept of rewarding positive patient outcomes versus tertiary savings based on formulary restrictions and impinging upon the prescribing authority of a physician.[4] A disempowered physician is likely to provide fewer medical services — including more aggressive use of innovative medical technologies, including diagnostics, devices and therapeutics. The increasing pressure of nonmedical budgetary constraints has a direct impact on the value of any given healthcare provider's lifetime of experience and hands-on patient contact.

Another foundational concept that is helping to propel the UAE's healthcare system forward is open, honest and regular communications with the various parts of their healthcare ecosystem. (See Figure 4.)

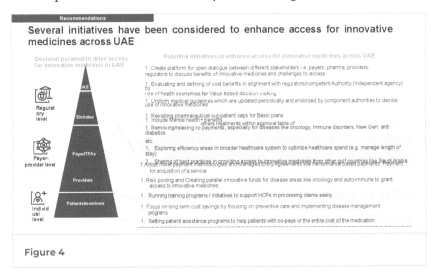

Figure 4

33

An important lesson is that dialogue counts. The UAE has been particularly good at managing an open-door policy with the innovative biopharmaceutical sector, maintaining a good dialogue with the industry on policies that could affect patients or the sector. And this extends to the emirate level, with Abu Dhabi setting up a new industry-government Advisory Council to collaborate on policies to boost investment, employment and innovation in the sector.[5] As per Dr. Farghaly, achieving "value over volume" is contingent on driving timely positive patient outcomes — and that's a team effort. "Value" as the denominator of the healthcare equation demands that multiple voices be heard — and heeded.

Lessons Learned from the COVID-19 Experience

"Value over volume" recognizes that, when it comes to advancing the public health, whether in the East, West or the Gulf Peninsula — we are all in this together. Get ready, world, the "Gulf Tiger" is poised for global leadership in the smart and savvy delivery of cost-effective, patient-focused healthcare.

REFERENCES

1. https://medicalinsurance.ae/wp-content/uploads/Health-Insurance-Law-English.pdf. Last accessed April 29, 2021.

2. https://duphat.ae/conference-program-2021/. Last accessed April 29, 2021.

3. https://www.ncbi.nlm.nih.gov/pmc/articles/PMC7693876/. Last accessed April 29, 2021.

4. https://scholar.google.com/scholar?q=Researches+about+improving+patient+care+and+outcomes&hl=en&as_sdt=0&as_vis=1&oi=scholart. Last accessed April 29, 2021.

5. https://bspace.buid.ac.ae/handle/1234/625. Last accessed April 29, 2021.

Government Detailing

By Peter J. Pitts

Originally published in *Drug Information Journal*, April 27, 2012

Abstract

"Newspeak," as Orwellian cognoscenti know, is the official language of Oceania — the land ruled by Big Brother. Newspeak was designed "not to extend but to diminish the range of thought." Its goal was to "make all other modes of thought impossible." All of which brings us from the nightmare fantasy of 1984 Newspeak to the healthcare debate of 2012, the concept of "academic detailing," and a new term we must all become familiar with — "cost-think" (which defines everything that reduces short-term costs as a benefit to the patient).

According to Dr. Jerry Avorn, professor of medicine at Harvard Medical School and chief of the Division of Pharmacoepidemiology, "Academic detailing is when healthcare professionals (usually pharmacists) meet with healthcare professionals to provide them with information and educational tools on various treatment options and optimal care, to improve provider knowledge of medical treatment effectiveness, encouraging alignment of practices with established evidence."[1] Left unsaid, but clearly implicit, is that such detailing is required to offset the free market doings of the pharmaceutical industry. That's why the more common appellation for academic detailing is counter detailing.

Why should anyone care? Well — not to put too fine a point on it — it's now the law of the land. Significant government funding has been provided to develop and roll out academic detailing programs. Our government is spending tens of millions of tax dollars to tell American physicians how to practice medicine based on comparative effectiveness studies that are commissioned without any public input or transparency. Additionally, the term "academic detailing" isn't accurate — because the work isn't being done by academics. It's government detailing — and the devil is in the details.

The Agency for Healthcare Research and Quality (AHRQ) hired a firm, Total Therapeutic Management, and is paying it US$11,680,060 to recruit and train physicians, pharmacists, nurses, and physician assistants.

We need to ask some tough but honest questions: Will physicians be required to be visited by this new battalion of government agents? Will physicians be given incentives to spend time with the Agency for Healthcare Research and Quality's angels — such as continuing medical education (CME credits) — and punished if they do not (via Medicare and Medicaid restrictions)?

A US$4 million "continuing education award" to Prime Education (an educational design and accreditation company focused on continuing medical education programs).

How will the government decide which doctors are to be visited? Will "high prescribers" of on-patent medicines be on a priority list? Barry Patel, the CEO of Total Therapeutic Management, said its top priority is "high volume" practices across 150 metropolitan statistical areas (MSAs) (interview with the author, February 2012). So, rather than focusing on offices with disproportionately high negative patient outcomes, the government is directing its efforts against those doctors who are high prescribers — which is a pretty good indicator about what government detailing is all about — decreasing cost rather than improving care.

As Harvard University health economist and healthcare advisor to President Obama, David Cutler, has noted, "Virtually every study of medical innovation suggests that changes in the nature of medical care over time are clearly worth the cost."[2] Access to care must be matched with quality of care. What safeguards are in place to certify that physicians are being presented information that is unbiased? Previous government detailing efforts have often focused on demonstrating their own value by highlighting the cost-effectiveness of initiatives through savings generated from the increased utilization of generics and other low-cost therapies.

When it comes to government detailing (at the taxpayers' expense), what are the metrics for success? According to Mr. Patel, the only metrics are whether or not a physician (1) says the sessions have been useful and (2) asks the detailer to come back to discuss other topics (interview with the author, February 2012). In other words, the metrics are subjective and anecdotal — but not clinical.

There is little information on why so few academic detailing programs attempt to measure overall healthcare cost reductions or improvement in patient outcomes. This is likely due to the fact that measuring changes in prescription drug costs is a more manageable analysis than determining changes in overall healthcare spending or clinical results. It also fits into the general cognitive mapping of those who believe that pharmaceutical costs are the main driver of healthcare costs. In fact, on-patent drug costs represent less than a dime on the American healthcare dollar.

Interestingly, Mr. Patel doesn't even agree with either the term "academic detailing" or "counter detailing." "We aren't counter anything. We're not there to un-do anything. It's not good versus bad... Our visits aren't details...they're the beginning of a process." And as far as "academic" goes,

Mr. Patel uses that term because that's the phrase AHRQ uses and placed in the contract. "Our people are patient-centered outcomes consultants, PCOCs," says Patel. And his people are largely pharmacists and nurses. A former Merck employee, Patel likens his PCOCs more to pharmaceutical company medical/science liaisons (MSLs) than field representatives. "They're not discussing product-specific information, but the findings of comparative effectiveness studies. Pharmaceutical companies could do the same thing if they wanted to" (interview with the author, February 2012).

Or could they? This can be argued either way, but in the current environment of regulatory oversight and political "sunshine," it is unlikely that any pharmaceutical company is going to risk "educating" physicians of comparative effectiveness studies. Nor will they be able to get physicians to grant them a scheduling slot with the promise of CME credits. According to Patel, when his "outreach experts" phone physicians to request appointments, the fact that the meeting will result in CME credits is always mentioned (interview with the author, February 2012). Would a pharmaceutical company be permitted to offer such an enticement? Would such an offer be "sunshine-able" under state and federal guidelines? And, if so, why don't government detailers have to share the details of their valued benefactions?

Interestingly, according to the Accreditation Council for Continuing Medical Education (ACCME), government is exonerated from having a commercial interest. (A commercial interest is any entity producing, marketing, reselling, or distributing healthcare goods or services consumed by, or used on, patients.) Our nation's single largest payer, Uncle Sam, is not deemed to have a conflict of interest when it comes to designing and providing physician CME.

In November 2011, at the International Conference on the Improved Use of Medicines in Antalya, Turkey, Elissa Ladd, a Massachusetts nurse-prescriber, spoke against the detailing practices of Big Pharma toward the growing population of nurse-prescribers. (According to Ms. Ladd, there are 150,000 nurse-prescribers in the US, compared with only 100,000 physicians in general practice.) You've heard the argument before — pharmaceutical detailing is "bad" because it helps to "sell" products for profit! She provided no evidence (anecdotal or otherwise) that the information pharmaceutical detailers provide to nurse-prescribers is in any way slanted or anything other than factual and 100 percent FDA-compliant.[4] Yet her organization undertook some "academic detailing" efforts that resulted in nurse-prescribers questioning the reliability of pharma-provided information. She positioned this as "success."[4] However, is having nurse-prescribers (or, for that matter, any prescriber) discount important vetted and timely medical information really a move in the right direction? That's more than an academic question.

Reducing the amount of money spent on drugs without improving the quality of care significantly limits the impact of detailing programs on overall healthcare costs. In fact, it just reinforces the concept of "fail first," a strategy that's good for payers — including the government, the nation's biggest payer — but bad for patient outcomes. A study fielded by the National Consumers League demonstrated that switching patients to less expensive generics doesn't always result in positive outcomes.

Consider that 15 percent of general prescription drug users say that they or a family member experienced therapeutic substitution, nearly half were dissatisfied (or their family was) with how the process occurred and report that this substitution did not result in lower out-of-pocket costs, and 40 percent said that the new medication was not as effective as the original one. What's more, nearly a third experienced more side effects following the substitution.

The repercussions of choosing short-term savings over long-term results, of cost-based choices over patient-centric care, of "fail first" policies over the right treatment for the right patient at the right time are pernicious to both the public purse and the public health.

Skimping on a more expensive medicine today but paying for an avoidable hospital stay later is a fool's errand.

And how can an "academic detailing" program funded by our nation's largest payer (the government) be considered neutral? Just like detailing programs run by pharmaceutical companies, there is an inherent "interest." Which is OK as long as that "interest" is transparent. But who will be the arbiters of transparency? Who will decide what these detailers can say or not say? Will these government "reps" have to play by the same rules as their pharmaceutical counterparts?

Most importantly, who will determine the difference between "communicating" these findings and "promoting" them? Alas, such finesse is unlikely under a regime of cost-think. As Orwell commented, Newspeak was constructed as to "give exact and often very subtle expression to every meaning that a Party member could properly wish to express, while excluding all other meanings and also the possibility or arriving at them by indirect methods."

US$18 million to Ogilvy Public Relations Worldwide, Healthcare Division to create a publicity center and another contract for US$8.6 million to create regional dissemination centers.

Importantly, what is the oversight mechanism? If academic detailers stray into off-label conversations, to whom does the FDA complain? Who does the Department of Justice investigate? Who pays the fine? Quis custodiet ipsos custodes? As currently designed, government detailing is a tool to increase government control over the practice of medicine and is a slippery slope toward the introduction of healthcare rationing and price controls. Congressional oversight must be required for the US$42.3 million that AHRQ has already awarded for public and physician outreach.

To maintain an even (and accountable) playing field, perhaps the AHRQ should adopt what is already law in the State of Maine. In 2007, the Pine Tree State passed a law to "establish a prescription drug academic detailing program... to enhance the health of residents of the State, to improve the quality of decisions regarding drug prescribing, to encourage better communication between the department and health care practitioners participating in publicly funded health programs and to reduce the health complications and unnecessary costs associated with inappropriate drug prescribing." Unlike the national program for government detailing, the Maine legislature included specific language regarding the oversight of educational materials:

> Academic detailers shall observe standards of conduct in their educa-
> tional materials and written and oral presentations as established by
> rules adopted by the department that are consistent with the follow-
> ing federal regulations regarding labeling and false and misleading
> advertising: the Food and Drug Administration labeling requirements
> of 21 Code of Federal Regulations, Part 201 (2007) and prescription
> drug advertising provisions of 21 Code of Federal Regulations, Part
> 202 (2007) and the Office of the Inspector General's Compliance
> Program Guidance for Pharmaceutical Manufacturers issued in April
> 2003, as amended.

As Rudyard Kipling said to the Royal College of Surgeons in London in 1923, "Words are, of course, the most powerful drug used by mankind. They enter into and colour the minutest cells of the brain." We allow them to be usurped and corrupted at our own peril.

The Recovery Act of 2010 (aka "the stimulus package") gave the Agency for Healthcare Research and Quality US$1.1 billion to conduct (according to the HHS press release)[8] "comparative effectiveness research" into various "healthcare interventions." However, that is not what Congress funded. Per the Recovery Act, that US$1.1 billion was earmarked for clinical compara-tive effectiveness, not comparative effectiveness research. This is not splitting hairs. Enter cost-think. Those in favor of comparative effectiveness research favor large-scale trials to "compare" drugs and other healthcare "technol-ogies, striving to show which medicines are most effective for any given disease state." Is there a "more effective" statin? A "more effective" treatment for depression? However, how does one compare two molecules (or three or more) that have different mechanisms of action for patients that respond differently to different medicine based on their personal genetic makeup?

Comparative effectiveness relies heavily on findings from randomized clinical trials. While these trials are essential to demonstrating the safety and efficacy of new medical products, the results are based on large population averages that rarely, if ever, will tell us which treatments are "best" for any given patient. Two such studies, the Clinical Antipsychotic Trials in Intervention Effectiveness (CATIE) study and the Antihypertensive and Lipid-Lowering Treatment to Prevent Heart Attack Trial (ALLHAT) study, were two such "practice based" clinical trials, sponsored in part by the National Institutes of Health, to determine whether older (cheaper) medicines were as effective in achieving certain clinical outcomes as newer (more expensive) ones. The findings of both CATIE and ALLHAT were highly controversial, but one thing is not: even well-funded comparative effectiveness trials are swiftly superseded by trial designs based on better mechanistic understanding of disease pathways and pharmacogenomics. Moreover, since most comparative effectiveness studies are underpowered, they don't capture the genetic variations that explain differences in response to medicines by different patients. Comparative effectiveness in its current form leads to a "one-size-fits-all" approach to healthcare, which means that it doesn't fit anyone particularly well.

Clinical effectiveness, on the other hand, measures outcomes on an individual patient level. Clinical effectiveness studies help us to understand how to design treatments based on patient variation rather than cost...the very definition of personalized medicine. As NIH Director Dr. Francis Collins warned the board of the Patient Centered Outcomes Research Institute (PCORI), "Beware of the tension between CER and personalized medicine" (PCORI board of directors meeting, May 2011).

In sum, the differences between comparative and clinical effectiveness studies are profound, and by changing the actual legislative verbiage, the legislative intent is likewise altered. The implications for academic detailing and crucial, since these are the very studies that will be detailed.

The Devil Is in the Detailing

As Orwell wrote, no word in the Newspeak vocabulary was "ideologically neutral" and a great many were "euphemisms." Welcome to cost-think, where anything that has to do with healthcare reform cannot be spoken about in terms of cost but must be entirely based on the philosophy of reducing short-term costs. Nowhere is cost-speak more crucial than when it comes to publicly bankrolled dissemination of the findings of taxpayer-bank-funded and AHRQ-fielded comparative effectiveness research. An important and honest question to ask is whether or not these studies will be peer-reviewed before they are allowed to be released. (CATIE and ALLHAT were not.) Government-sponsored comparative effectiveness research, communicated through government detailing, is the first step toward allowing our government to push a restrictive formulary on more and more Americans. Unless we are aware and vigilant, such cost-think may very well lead to a single-payer system referred to in cost-think as "universal coverage." In reality, however, it will be nothing short of healthcare rationing. Government detailing is the razor-sharp tip of the spear.

Intent Dissent

What makes the FDA's Dr. Bob Temple so endearing (and his opinions so enduring) is his blunt truth telling. At a recent conference hosted by the National Pharmaceutical Council and cosponsored by the National Health Council and WellPoint ("Asymmetry in the Ability to Communicate CER Findings: Ethics and Issues for Informed Decision Making"; February 9, 2012. Washington, DC), he stated his belief that regulations on product promotion should not impede companies from rebutting findings from comparative effectiveness research involving their products. This may not initially sound that important, but it's a clarion call for those who understand the imperative to systematically and scientifically counter the counter-detailing efforts coming thanks to the tens of millions of tax dollars earmarked for such efforts by the Patient Protection and Affordable Care Act (PPACA).

According to the *Pink Sheet*,[9] "The subject of asymmetry in the reporting and commenting on CER findings has been a key point of discussion for [the National Pharmaceutical Council] as CER has taken on a more visible role within the health care debate. Some suggest manufacturers of products subject to CER might have difficulty discussing the findings of the research given FDA restraints on commercial speech." Perhaps not. Speaking at the February 9 conference, Dr. Temple said there is "no FDA view... that drug companies are condemned to silence about their products outside of formal promotion or perhaps published articles. If there's something published that seems wrong, is based on poorly designed meta-analysis and so on, I don't see any impediment to answer that and companies do answer that all the time."

Indeed, Temple seemed surprised and displeased that industry has sat by while leading proponents of comparative effectiveness share their questionable conclusions. He commented as follows: "A recent example might be newspaper assertions that antidepressants have no long-term benefit and really don't work. This has been published repeatedly, and I'd like to see a rebuttal from the people who make antidepressants, because I think the published reports... are wrong. [FDA] may get around to rebutting, but somebody else might want to, and I don't think there is any impediment to doing that."

It should be noted that Temple qualified his remarks by saying (appropriately) that companies should be mindful of how FDA regulates speech when (and if) they decide to rebut wrong or misleading information from a comparative effectiveness research (whether or not it's government funded). "It is clear to me that a sponsor could correct or dispute a CER statement by a payer, or even the government, as long as the correction was not itself promotional." Which prompts the question, what precisely does "promotional" mean, and who is to judge? Temple gives a good example of how to avoid such a problem: "In recent months, we've seen companies disagree publicly with meta-analyses, with epidemiologic conclusions they considered unsupported on methodologic grounds, and that's OK, although making their own [conclusions] probably would not be." In other words, it's not "promotional" to point out a comparative effectiveness study's design flaws and, therefore, the errors of its conclusions. If such an approach is "compliant," it opens up tremendous opportunity in countering so called "academic" detailing.

However, while Temple's is a powerful voice inside the FDA, it is only one voice. If Secretary Sebelius's interference in the agency's Plan B decision is any indication — might not his view be similarly overturned by the mandarins in the Humphrey Building? After all, the comparative effectiveness studies under debate are funded by PPACA and fielded by AHRQ. Moreover, the current administration has not looked kindly on those who question either its philosophical motives or legislative methods. Industry is deemed guilty until proven guilty. The current modus operandi seems to follow Franz Kafka's statement that "My guiding principle is this: Guilt is never to be doubted."

Which brings us back to the question, what does promotional mean? A recent paper by Coleen Klasmeier, a former FDA attorney and currently the head of Sidley Austin's FDA regulatory practice, addresses this issue head-on.[10] She observed that "The FDA approach is one of delicate balance — of forbidding off-label promotion without undue incursion into the ability of physicians to obtain information about off-label uses from manufacturers." This issue of "undue incursion" seems to dovetail nicely with Temple's notion of focusing on design flaws and incorrect conclusions. But what of intent? Intent is in the eyes of the beholder. Where one person might see a robust discussion of study design, another might see promotional intent. The foundational problem, as Klasmeier eloquently pointed out, is the FDA's reliance on "multifactorial tests rather than bright-line standards".[10]

Plainly stated, regulators at the FDA (and particularly those who must address thorny First Amendment issues) embrace ambiguity over predictability. It gives them almost limitless power. Industry, on the other hand, wants and needs an evidence-based regulatory framework that provides predictable standards for their communications efforts. Bright lines. Predictability is power in pursuit of the public health. Minus such an effort, we get the troubling example of Par Pharmaceutical. In a pending First Amendment suit against the FDA,[11] Par contends the government is criminalizing its speech to healthcare professionals about the on-label use of its appetite suppressant Megacel ES (megestrol acetate) in settings where doctors prescribe the drug for both approved and unapproved uses. Par's complaint, filed October 14 in the US District Court for the District of Columbia, seeks a preliminary injunction against government enforcement of FDA labeling regulations on the grounds they are harming Par's First Amendment rights by chilling protected speech.

Par's suit states that physicians more frequently prescribe the drug to treat wasting in non-AIDS geriatric and cancer patients and that the majority of prescriptions for the drug are for off-label uses. Par also seeks a declaratory judgment that it may speak about the approved use to physicians who could prescribe it for that use, even if they are more likely to prescribe the drug for off-label uses. "Common sense dictates that the government cannot justify censoring a broad swath of truthful and valuable speech regarding lawful activity out of a desire to prevent other lawful activity," a memorandum in support of the motion for preliminary injunction states. "And it is absurd to think that the government may imprison a person for engaging in truthful speech about a lawful activity that the government itself subsidizes."

At issue in Par's suit are provisions in the Food, Drug, and Cosmetic Act concerning "intended use" of a drug and misbranding. "If a manufacturer speaks about the on-label use of its drug in a setting where the manufacturer knows that physicians prescribe the drug off-label, the government interprets the FDA's 'intended use' regulations to deem the manufacture to be expressing an 'objective intent' that physicians prescribe the drug off-label," Par's memorandum states. In a press release announcing the suit,[12] Par said it hoped to "elicit tailored and constitutionally permissible regulatory guidance to ensure that physicians may be kept abreast of valuable, on-label information about prescription drugs to aid in their provision of quality and informed patient care."

If a company can be challenged when it discusses strictly on-label uses of a product, how much more convoluted, challenging, and intimidating will it be to challenge a government-funded and government-detailed comparative effectiveness study? Disputing comparative effectiveness studies, or any research, need not fall into the chasm of promotion (off-label or otherwise). To lump scientific discourse into this slippery silo is to court both agency action and political attention. As Klasmeier[10] noted, "The off-label problem reflects the accretion of administrative interpretations over the years...the commercialization of an investigational new drug is not to be construed to interfere with a manufacturer's entitlement to engage in scientific exchange."

Is it not the case that debating the flaws of a research study scientific exchange, even if (and especially when) such exchanges raise questions about conclusions that are contrary to any given company's marketing and sales objectives? How does the issue of intent play into compliance when legitimate scientific exchanges also impact promotional considerations? On which side should regulators err? The answer is as easy as it is difficult — regulators should err on the side of the public health. Perhaps the best precedent is FDAMA Section 401, which expressly permits companies to provide reprints of peer-reviewed medical journal articles on off-label studies (as long as they have a pending supplemental application with the agency).

Let us remember the astute observation of William Blake that, "A truth that's told with bad intent, beats all the lies you can invent." To paraphrase Douglas MacArthur, "The patient, and the patient, and the patient."

REFERENCES

1. Soumerai SB, Avorn J. Principles of educational outreach ("academic detailing") to improve clinical decision making. JAMA. 1990;263(4):549–556.

2. Cutler DM. Use a scalpel, not a meat cleaver [essay response]. Cato Unbound. September 12, 2007. http://www.cato-unbound.org/2007/09/12/david-m-cutler/use-a-scalpel-not-a-meat-cleaver/. Accessed April 2012.

3. Accreditation Council for Continuing Medical Education (ACCME). Definition of a commercial interest. http://www.accme.org/requirements/accreditation-requirements-cme-providers/policies-and-definitions/definition-commercial-interest.

4. Ladd E. Presentation at: Third International Conference for Improving Use of Medicines; November 10, 2011; Antalya, Turkey.

5. National Consumers League Web site. http://www.nclnet.org/health/42-drug-substitution. Accessed March 2012.

6. Piepho RW. Therapeutic interchange and equivalence: focus on antihypertensive agents Medscape Web site. http://www.medscape.org/viewarticle/416390_4. Accessed March 2012.

7. Sec. 1. 22 MRSA c. 603, sub-c. 1-A.http://www.mainelegislature.org/ros/LOM/lom123rd/PUBLIC327.asp.

8. US Department of Health & Human Services. Federal Coordinating Council for Comparative Effectiveness Research: Report to the President and the Congress. www. hhs.gov/recovery/programs/cer/cerannualrpt.pdf. Published June 30, 2009. Accessed March 2012.

9. Sutter S. Will FDA's view on health economic claims change with more government-funded research? The Pink Sheet. 2012;47(9). http://www.elsevierbi.com/Publications/ The-Pink-Sheet/74/9/Will-!FDAs-View-On-Health-Economic-Claims-Change-With MoreGovernmentFundedResearch?result¼1&total¼1335&searchquery¼%253fq %253dTemple. Accessed March 21, 2012.

10. Klasmeier C. FDA regulation of off-label promotion: an answer. Social Science Research Network (SSRN). Published February 5, 2012. http://ssrn.com/abstract=2000329.

11. Par Pharmaceutical, Inc. v United States of America et al. Case number 1:2011cv01820. Filed October 14, 2011.

12. Par Pharmaceutical files declaratory judgment to protect First Amendment rights to disseminate truthful information regarding Megace1 ES [press release]. Woodcliff Lake, NJ, October 14, 2011. http://investors.parpharm.com/phoenix. zhtml?c=81806&p=irol-newsArticle&ID=1617464&highlight.

Reconsidering the 21st-Century FDA

"Silent gratitude isn't very much use to anyone." GERTRUDE STEIN

America's response to COVID-19 would have been impossible without the superhuman efforts of the men and women of the US Food & Drug Administration (FDA) but the thank-yous have been few and far between. So be it. There were many regulatory lessons learned during the pandemic, not the least of which is that when the FDA is an ally in advancing innovation, public health is the victor. These learnings can and must be applied to every aspect of the agency's mission. But is the FDA moving too fast or too slow? Oftentimes, where you stand on this issue depends on where you sit in the healthcare ecosystem. Can't we all just get along?

Too Fast or Too Slow: Is the FDA Moving at the Right Speed?

By Peter J. Pitts

Originally published in *Health Affairs*, March 19, 2021

Regardless of President Joe Biden's choice for the next commissioner of the Food and Drug Administration (FDA), the Senate Health, Education, Labor and Pensions Committee will likely pose one question above all others to the nominee: Is the FDA approving drugs too quickly or too slowly?

As someone who has seen the FDA from the inside as an associate commissioner, I can attest to the tremendous pride that the agency takes in the thoughtful, savvy, and swift introduction of new medicines through the review process. The FDA employs new tools and techniques of regulatory science, with the end result of bringing important new medications to market quickly. The expedited pathways introduced by the FDA that incorporate new uses of data collection and regulatory science are a potent tool in America's public health armamentarium. Speedier review has resulted in more drugs for serious and life-threatening diseases, with solid benefit/risk profiles. In short, the speed with which the FDA moves saves lives.

Regulatory Dimensionality

Who decides what is the appropriate benefit/risk calculation? According to former FDA Commissioner Robert Califf, MD, when there is a life-threatening disease with no effective treatment, "patient groups have been very clear that they are willing to take a high degree of risk to have earlier access." FDA divisional staff, to their credit, have embraced this approach. It reflects what I call regulatory dimensionality.

Despite well-meaning voices to the contrary, there is no evidence to support the notion that the FDA is approving everything; or that every product that requests an expedited pathway receives it; or that all those that do receive an expedited pathway designation get approved; or that every product that does reach the market via an expedited approval in some way provides less benefit to patients than other medicines.

Critics should consider the recent case of Merck and its voluntary withdrawal of Keytruda for its metastatic small-cell lung cancer indication, which was approved via accelerated approval in 2019. This is a strong, recent example of how innovators and the FDA can and do regularly collaborate to balance benefits and risks as new data become available. Merck's action comes as part of an industrywide evaluation by the FDA of drugs that do not meet the post-marketing checkpoints on which their accelerated approvals were granted. It reinforces the FDA's promised vigilance in following up on products reviewed via its various facilitated pathways and holding sponsors to their post-marketing commitments. Only 6 percent of accelerated approvals for oncology indications have been withdrawn.

When it comes to oncology drugs, speed to market is literally a life-or-death calculation. In May 2017, the FDA issued a press release announcing that they had "granted accelerated approval to a treatment for patients whose cancers have a specific genetic feature (biomarker). This is the first time the agency has approved a cancer treatment based on a common biomarker rather than the location in the body where the tumor originated."

"This is an important first for the cancer community," said FDA's Richard Pazdur, MD, after his team approved a drug based on a tumor's biomarker without regard to the location. This was viewed as a win for the FDA and a win for patients. But what is not so readily visible are the difficult and risky decisions required by both the agency and the developer. The savvy and strategic use of new regulatory tools saves lives. So, it would not be appropriate to say that the FDA has been too fast in making these determinations.

In fact, the FDA has been very selective. Looking at the record of the FDA's various expedited pathways: Of the 364 requests for Breakthrough Therapy designation from July 2012 to June 2016, the Center for Drug Evaluation and Research (CDER) at the FDA only granted 133 (37 percent) of those requests. The CDER denied 182 (50 percent), and the sponsor withdrew their request 49 times (13 percent) before the agency made a decision.

In other cases, the FDA has provided important clinical benefits to patients sooner: Among 22 drugs with 24 indications granted accelerated approval by the FDA between 2009 and 2013, 42 percent had efficacy confirmed in post-approval trials a minimum of three years after approval. Confirmatory trials and preapproval trials had similar design elements, including reliance on surrogate measures as outcomes. Therefore, it would be unfair to say that the FDA is approving unsafe, ineffective, or dangerous drugs.

Follow the Data
The agency's review pathways must be constantly reviewed with vigilance. Neither the FDA nor those tasked with oversight of its activities can afford to allow regulatory stasis to allow "review drift." Instead, data should map the way.

In April, the FDA's Oncology Drugs Advisory Committee will review six indications for Roche's Tecentriq (atezolizumab), Merck's Keytruda (pembrolizumab), and Bristol Myers Squibb's Opdivo (nivolumab) in breast, urothelial, gastric, and hepatocellular cancers. The committee will receive updates on the results of the confirmatory trials and the status of any ongoing or planned trials for each indication and will be tasked with making recommendations on whether the indications should remain approved while additional trials are conducted.

Per Pazdur, "We are committed to ensuring the integrity of the accelerated approval program, which is designed to bring safe and effective drugs to patients with unmet medical needs as quickly as possible. The program allows the FDA to approve a drug or biologic product intended to treat a serious or life-threatening condition based on an outcome that can be measured earlier than survival that demonstrates a meaningful advantage over available therapies. However, when confirmatory trials do not confirm clinical benefit, a reevaluation must be performed to determine if the approval should be withdrawn." Pazdur added that the meeting will give outside experts and patients a chance to provide input to the agency on how it should proceed with each indication.

The FDA is rightly embracing regulatory dimensionality, by which I mean a combination of scrupulous review processes and pragmatism. Together with a recalibrated sense of regulatory velocity, this is the agency's next step toward a more patient-centric and innovative (aka, modern) regulatory attitude. The FDA will be seen as an innovation accelerator — precisely the legislative clarion call of the bipartisan 21st Century Cures Act, and a characterization that the next FDA chief nominee ought to embrace.

Importantly, it is critical to understand that new approaches to clinical programs and shorter review via expedited review pathways do not mean a less rigorous FDA interrogation of the data. It means a different, yet scientifically rigorous, approach with different roles and responsibilities on the part of both agency and sponsor and acknowledging the needs and preferences of patients living with serious diseases. And it will almost certainly mean more time, effort, and expense in the postmarket environment.

As now Acting FDA Commissioner Janet Woodcock, MD, said in April 2016, "Failing to approve a drug that actually works in devastating diseases — these consequences are extreme." Doing things in new ways with new tools is always challenging, and political headwinds can be fierce.

President Biden's choice for FDA commissioner comes at a crucial moment in the history of 21st-century drug discovery and regulatory science. When it comes time for this nominee to answer the "too fast or too slow" question, patients already have their answer — more drugs reviewed more swiftly through the use of sound 21st-century science is a great leap forward in the agency's mission. They hope the nominee agrees.

Should We Rethink the FDA Commissionership?

By Peter J. Pitts

Originally published in *Health Affairs*, December 22, 2021

The U.S. Food and Drug Administration prides itself on being, first and foremost, all about science. So, how did the agency that regulates upwards of 30 percent of the U.S. economy get so caught up in tacking against biting political crosswinds? As a veteran of the regulatory wars, I believe the rocky seas began to roil when the position of FDA Commissioner became Senate confirmable in 1988. Prior to 1988, FDA Commissioners were appointed by the Secretary of HHS and thus not subject to Senate confirmation. To be sure, Senate confirmation certainly adds importance to the position of FDA Commissioner, and it brings the nominee into intimate contact with many members of Congress. That's a positive. But the system of "holds" whereby senators haggle and bargain with the Commissioner-Designate over various matters is unseemly, if not improper.

Since 1988, addressing tough scientific and public policy issues has become even more difficult as the Commissioner now must often deflect the often politically motivated slings and arrows of elected officials. Dr. David Kessler, the second Senate-confirmed FDA Commissioner, made national headlines with his controversial efforts to regulate tobacco. More recent politicized issues include the approvals of Mifepristone ("the abortion pill"), Plan B ("the morning after pill"), Exondys 51 (for Duchenne's Muscular Dystrophy), Aduhelm (for Alzheimer's Disease), and policy issues such as drug importation, expanded access to experimental medicines (and related state and federal "Right-to-Try" legislation), medical marijuana, cannabidiol (CBD), and the more aggressive use of expedited drug review pathways. The current debate over the FDA's COVID-19 Emergency Use Authorizations and other related decisions have undermined public confidence in the agency at a time when faith in our public health institutions is crucial in advancing our battle against the pandemic.

When one considers the FDA's mission—to independently protect consumers and advance the public health—it is not at all clear whether the Commissioner should "serve at the pleasure of the President." Perhaps a better idea is for the Commissioner to be nominated by the President for a fixed 6-year term—like that of the Director of the FBI. Think about it—why should the safety of food additives, the integrity of the blood and vaccine supply, and decisions on drug labeling indications (to name only a few FDA responsibilities) be considered Democratic or Republican issues? The boss of the FDA Commissioner is and should continue to be the Secretary of Health and Human Services—a politically appointed, Senate-confirmed cabinet officer – just as the Director of the FBI reports to the Attorney General. More politics just leads to regulatory paralysis and discord—neither which protects or advances America's health.

Now, consider going a step further: Perhaps the FDA Commissioner and other like positions should be remodeled after the British model of a permanent under-secretary. In the United Kingdom, permanent secretaries are the non-political civil service heads or "chief executives of government departments, who generally hold their position for a number of years (thus "permanent") at a ministry as distinct from the changing ministers of state to whom they report and provide advice.

British permanent secretaries are appointed under a scheme in which the Prime Minister has the final say in the recruitment process. The resident of 10 Downing Street chooses directly from a list created by non-partisan Civil Service Commissioners. A new structure for choosing future FDA Commissioners would begin by creating a panel of Public Health Commissioners. This won't be easy – but bold and important steps rarely are. It could also be a model for other leadership appointments.

Ultimately, our goal should be for the person chosen as FDA Commissioner to serve as free of the political current as possible and selection of career public health officials should not be dismissed out of hand.

To be sure, taking my reasoning even further might lead one to ask: if insulating the Commissioner from politics is a good thing, then why not create a tenured "lifetime" Commissioner in the style of a Supreme Court or Federal Justice? Yet, even the most dedicated and brilliant person ultimately becomes a prisoner of the status quo. A regular and robust challenging of regulatory customs and circumstances is required. A "that's not the way we do things here" attitude at the FDA is already a burden and barrier to innovation. Let's not solve one problem only to create a more dangerous one.

Having had the honor to serve our country and our President as an FDA Associate Commissioner, I can unequivocally state that the unwelcome infusion of politics into science makes an already difficult job that much more difficult. Worse still, to have the job of Commissioner open and only partially filled for extended lengths of time grinds progress to a halt. Low morale, lengthy delays, and even postponements often characterize an open Commissionership. Lengthy acting commissionerships have become the rule rather than the exception. This is not acceptable.

A 6-year fixed term would mean no gap in a "confirmed" Commissioner between presidential administrations. And de-politicizing the selection process via a standing panel of public health commissioners would further strengthen the foundation and reputation of the FDA as an institution free of political influence.

Such changes represent a long and arduous policy objective. In the near term, policy makers should confirm the next FDA Commissioner expeditiously. Doing so is important to advancing the American public health and an important indication of the seriousness with which President Biden and the United States Senate takes this position – and the FDA as a whole. Let's hope it's done swiftly and smartly.

REFERENCES

1. https://www.congress.gov/bill/100th-congress/senate-bill/2889
2. https://www.pbs.org/wgbh/pages/frontline/shows/settlement/interviews/kessler.html
3. https://www.plannedparenthood.org/planned-parenthood-pacific-southwest/blog/mifepristone-anniversary-of-fda-approval
4. http://commercialbiotechnology.com/index.php/jcb/article/view/600
5. https://journals.sagepub.com/doi/full/10.1177/2168479018774556
6. https://www.realclearhealth.com/articles/2021/07/18/aduhelm_lessons_from_its_approval__111229.html
7. https://www.fda.gov/patients/learn-about-expanded-access-and-other-treatment-options/right-try
8. https://www.fda.gov/news-events/public-health-focus/fda-regulation-cannabis-and-cannabis-derived-products-including-cannabidiol-cbd
9. https://www.healthaffairs.org/do/10.1377/hblog20210317.69490/full/
10. https://www.npr.org/2020/09/25/917014322/trust-in-cdc-and-fda-is-at-a-low
11. https://www.gov.uk/government/organisations/civil-service/about/our-governance#permanent-secretaries

FDA Needs a Competitiveness Czar

By Peter J. Pitts

Originally published in *Health Affairs*, October, 15, 2021

The FDA needs a Deputy Commissioner for Regulatory Competitiveness. The "why" is obvious — too many health policy experts, medical product developers and investors view the Food and Drug Administration as a hindrance to innovation. They see the agency as slow, risk averse, and unpredictable. But the FDA can (and, indeed, must) become an innovation accelerator and a competitiveness enabler.

Reporting directly to the FDA Commissioner, the Deputy Commissioner for Regulatory Competitiveness would aggressively develop, coordinate, and drive agency initiatives that allow new medical products and technologies to come to market faster and less expensively — without sacrificing sound regulatory science. The Deputy Commissioner would help to ensure that therapeutic monopolies are not allowed to continue years after patent expiry and that regulatory ambiguity (across the entire portfolio of FDA responsibilities) would not stymie investment or innovation.

This would be a cross-functional position that would work across all agency centers and other assets of the Department of Health and Human Services (CMS, NIH, CDC, etc.) to drive competition through smart policy development, process enhancement, and resource allotment. The Deputy Commissioner should engage with regulated industries and other interested parties as a "Regulatory Competitiveness Czar," collecting valuable ideas, aspirations, concrete recommendations (and even arguments against) ways to make the FDA a leader and driver of a more competitiveness-friendly regulation.

Competitiveness Score

The first step toward a Competitiveness Designation would be a score of 4 or greater on an *FDA Competitiveness Score.* This new "C-Score" would rank product applications (generic, nonbiologic complex drug, drug, biologic, biosimilar, medical device, combination product, vaccine, etc.) that have the potential to impact free-market forces within a therapeutic category. A good score on this metric could lead to a *Competitiveness Designation,* providing a product with an expedited review pathway similar to those currently offered for advances in specific advances in therapeutic care. As the current expedited pathways reward and incentivize investment in targeted therapeutic areas, the aim of the proposed Competitiveness Designation would be to incentivize development programs that significantly impact the free-market dynamics of the healthcare marketplace, thereby enabling marketplace competitiveness. Examples of such products might include a generic alternative to corticotrophin (a very high-cost product that is off-patent but has no generic alternatives) and chemically synthesized insulin analogues.

The Competitiveness Designation would be based on a 1-5 Competitiveness Index Score (with 1 being the lowest and 5 the highest) developed by the FDA and relevant stakeholders. The score would be a first step to identify an aggressively competitive product from a less competitive one. One variable could be the total cost of disease on our national healthcare resources (both public and private).

As a benefit of securing a Competitiveness Designation, FDA could: offer additional FDA resources; facilitate and expedite a parallel FDA/CMS review; provide a "Competitiveness Voucher" to be used or sold (similar to the CDER/CBER voucher program). A Competitiveness Designation would not in any way impact any review division decisions (safety/efficacy, clinical trial design, labeling language, etc.).

The mission of the Deputy Commissioner for Regulatory Competitiveness is to steer the FDA toward faster, less costly reviews, more aggressive anti-monopolistic actions, and smart and directive regulatory policies that recognize and incorporate practical free-market principles. The Deputy Commissioner for Regulatory Competitiveness must have an intimate knowledge of how the FDA works and personal relationships with its senior leadership so that progress can be made quickly and, ultimately, institutionalized. The Deputy Commissioner must know how to work both within and outside system, how to build alliances, and how to avoid becoming marginalized in the very byzantine world of FDA process and internal politics.

The Cures Act

Why "regulatory competitiveness"? The 21st Century Cures Act has empowered the FDA to use new science to speed product development and review. It also directs the agency to advance and evolve how the products under its jurisdiction are measured for both safety and effectiveness once approved and on the market. But the uptake of new pathways and tools has been slow and uneven. What senior agency management says publicly about the value and urgency of regulatory innovation has yet to take root in its product review divisions, creating doubt across the broader healthcare ecosystem that the FDA can be a potent ally in lowering costs and advancing patient access to new and important medical technologies. The Deputy Commissioner for Regulatory Competitiveness will demonstrate the agency's commitment to both the letter and spirit of the 21st Century Cures Act.

As W. Edwards Deming reminds us, "What we need to do is learn to work in the system. Every team, every platform, every division, every component is there for contribution to the system as a whole on a win-win basis." In short, the FDA must not only strive to be an *innovation accelerator* but also a *competitiveness enabler.*

A Breakthrough for Alzheimer's Patients — And a Need for More

By Peter J. Pitts

Originally published in *International Business Times*, August 14, 2021

The FDA just approved a new Alzheimer's medication for the first time in nearly two decades. The drug, aducanumab, could potentially slow patients' cognitive decline. This is a medical innovation of the first order.

And yet, this tremendous breakthrough has led to some ignorant hand wringing. Detractors are questioning the drug's clinical effectiveness and balking at its $56,000 list price.

These critics misunderstand the staggering clinical hardships and economic burden of Alzheimer's disease — and the approval itself, which was only granted on a conditional basis. The FDA should be applauded for its use of 21st-century regulatory science. It also makes sound financial sense.

The growing prevalence of Alzheimer's disease is a frightening national emergency. The disease afflicts 6.2 million Americans, a number expected to more than double by 2060. It is already one of the top 10 causes of death in the United States. By greenlighting aducanumab, which is administered via a once-a-month intravenous injection, the FDA has given patients with mild cognitive impairment or early dementia something that yesterday's patients' didn't have: hope.

That is worth plenty in and of itself. But the approval can also help address the economic cost of Alzheimer's disease, which threatens to swamp the US healthcare system. Treating Alzheimer's currently costs more than $305 billion a year. That figure will likely exceed $1 trillion by 2050 unless new treatments or cures are developed, according to a study published in the *American Journal of Managed Care*. A medicine that slows cognitive decline will significantly help rein in these costs.

Will it work? The FDA granted accelerated approval to aducanumab for its ability to clear amyloid, a form of plaque that develops on patients' brains. By clearing these plaques, the drug may deliver the kind of cognitive benefits that previous treatments have failed to provide. Under the accelerated approval process, aducanumab's maker, Biogen, is required to conduct a new effectiveness trial. If the company can't demonstrate cognitive benefits, the FDA could reverse its decision.

The Accelerate Approval Program, often used for innovative cancer treatments, "can bring therapies to patients faster while spurring more research and innovation," according to the director of the FDA's Center for Drug Evaluation and Research.

Critics of the FDA decision are correct to point out that uncertainties remain. Welcome to science! We have to embrace innovation while also monitoring products in the real world to ensure they maintain a solid benefit/risk profile. That is exactly what's happening. Kudos to the FDA for choosing the course of action with the most potential upside for Alzheimer's patients, their families, and our health system as a whole.

Some pundits and politicians have also criticized the drug's price, with some even using this high list price to drum up support for a drug-pricing bill. That bill, known as H.R. 3, would cap prices on a wide range of new drugs, with limits based on prices paid in other developed countries.

But this is the wrong response to the Alzheimer's crisis. More than anything, patients need sustained progress toward better treatments. Importing foreign price controls, as H.R. 3 does, would slash drug-company revenues and discourage firms from funding new research into Alzheimer's and other serious and life-threatening diseases.

Medical innovation isn't cheap. It costs more than $2.5 billion to create just one new drug, after all. But in the case of Alzheimer's — a potentially $1 trillion-a-year epidemic — the cost of inaction far exceeds the cost of progress.

Judging from their decision to move ahead with aducanumab, FDA officials understand this. Given the scope and severity of the Alzheimer's crisis, the agency made the right choice.

Settling for Second Best?

By Peter J. Pitts

Originally published in *Nature Biotechnology*, July 2007

To the Editor:

Your editorial "Probity gone nuts" (Nat. Biotechnol. 25, 483, 2007) hits the nail on the head with the statement, "The thinking behind the FDA's draft guidance on financial conflicts of interest for outside experts is deeply flawed." But there are more nails that need to be hammered in pursuit of public health.

As I've said elsewhere, all those who naively call for a "conflict-free code" for US Food and Drug Administration (FDA) advisory committee members don't comprehend that such a zero-tolerance policy would lead to the destruction of the most open, transparent — and successful — program of clinical review in the world. Consider Canada and Europe where advisory committees meet in secret, deliberating behind closed doors, commenting publicly only after they have reached a decision.

During my time at the FDA, I was the senior official in charge of advisory committees. I recollect a meeting with officials from Health Canada — the FDA's equivalent in Ottawa — who were aghast that our advisory committee meetings were regularly attended by members of the media, financial analysts, patient groups, and politicians — and that the meetings were recorded for public consumption.

I explained that such transparency was what made the meetings so valuable. When any FDA advisory committee is in session, the agency is put to the test, to explain and defend its scientific thinking in public, before a panel of experts with the breadth and depth of experience to dissect the results, to challenge conclusions and to make sure that no clinical stone goes unturned.

And the cornerstones of every advisory committee are the clinical experts who serve on them. The best and the brightest our nation has to offer.

But as FDA Deputy Commissioner Scott Gottlieb said to me, the value of these meetings could be eroded "if current legislative proposals become law and FDA is hampered in its ability to put experience and expertise as the paramount criteria when recruiting members to serve on these committees." He was rightly concerned by those Monday-morning regulators "who want appearance to trump acumen — who want the lack of private sector work to trump a plethora of scientific experience as a criterion when we are selecting who to put on our committees." This is mania winning over measure, with the most recent example being the FDA's own recommended restrictions — the infamous $50,000 rule. Why is an expert conflicted at $50,000, but not at $49,999.99? There are many things wrong with what the agency has proposed — most of all that it is driven by politics rather than sound science (although I predict as many waivers tomorrow as today, because at the end of the day the career FDA medical staff will demand the best and the brightest).

Commenting on a panel discussion last year on government-sponsored advisory committees[1] organized by the Center for Science in the Public Interest (CSPI; Washington, DC, USA) — a group whose regular criticism of the agency makes Charles Grassley's aureate prattle look meek by comparison — I noted then the remarks of Scott Gottlieb: "It would be a significant step backwards if our primary criterion for selecting members to our committees becomes their lack of private sector work, if we exclude people for deep experience rather than embrace them for it. The public health will not be served if we're no longer able to attract the kind of very active medical practitioners and clinical realists who are able to inform our meetings with some very unique medical insights that only come from years of experience both seeing patients and developing and looking at clinical data, sometimes in some very narrow fields or for specific indications."

But as I have noted before,[1] "agency critics continue to ask simplistic questions, phrased more like accusations than inquiries. For example, 'Why can't the FDA just appoint panels with experts who don't have conflicts and, therefore, won't need waivers?' It sounds good as a sound bite, but even a little homework shows the ignorance inherent in the question. FDA doesn't appoint advisory committee members meeting-by-meeting, case-by-case, action-by-action. FDA advisory committees are standing committees, with members recruited and appointed sometimes years in advance, and who serve for defined terms of up to four years." And, according to Gottlieb, "this serves us well, since there is a value from having people who have institutional experience from serving on these committees. It is similar to the way the Senate works, where you don't want all the members being brand new each year, or appointed just to vote on each individual issue."

And, as Gottlieb reminded the CSPI panel last year "this leads me to the heart of the problem: when we appoint these committee members, it is impossible to tell who is going to have relationships that could present the potential for an appearance of a conflict around a specific issue, and therefore require them to get a waiver, since we don't know what issues are going to come up a year or two in advance. If we err on the side of caution, and only appoint members who have had absolutely no associations of any kind with any regulated products or industries, then we're going to be hard pressed to find people that have also been engaged in relevant and unique scientific endeavors, since a lot of medical product research is done in collaboration, at least in part, with sponsors."

He went on: "If we were prevented from being able to grant waivers in the first place, we'd have to recruit people who had no such associations, and were unlikely to develop them for the length of their tenure on our committees. I'm not only worried that such people would be very hard for us to find, especially since it's sometimes not obvious to researchers themselves that their institution might have received a grant for research they had no involvement in, or a clinical trial they are working on might have received partial funding from a private source."

I wondered at that time,[1] "Might we really pass legislation that bans the best and the brightest from serving the public health by disallowing their service on advisory committees because their preeminent expertise has also been viewed as valuable by the pharmaceutical industry?"

And, when it comes to transparency — shouldn't it be applied to everyone involved in the process? Why is it that only some groups need to be transparent? In many of today's news reports on the FDA's new draft guidance on advisory committee conflict of interest some groups are deemed "consumer advocates." No mention is made of their funding sources, whereas other individuals are quoted with the tag "industry funded." And what about advisory committee members who have served as "expert" witnesses in court trials against pharmaceutical companies? Often such fees are in excess of $50,000, but such rewards are not mentioned by either the FDA or various and sundry pieces of legislation.

Finally, as I wrote online,[1] "I can attest, as a former senior FDA official, that it is very difficult to recruit the best and the brightest. The proposed guidance would make it almost impossible. After all, who would want to serve on an advisory committee when you're viewed as a potential criminal before the ink on your appointment is even dry? Independent-thinking advisory committee members will feel threatened and suffocated by the unspoken threat of federal investigators knocking at their clinic doors. Such legislation amounts to advisory committee lettres de cachet for folks like the CSPI, posturing politicians and Page One hungry reporters."

REFERENCES

1. http://drugwonks.com/2006/07/process_not_persecution.html.

Biosimilars: Strength vs. Potency: Avoiding a Regulatory Hobson's Choice

By Peter J. Pitts

Originally published in *Food and Drug Law Institute*, September 2021

Introduction

The US Food and Drug Administration's (FDA) current interpretation of "strength" does not allow a biological product to be licensed as a biosimilar and/or interchangeable product if there is any variation in inactive drug volume, even if it has the same amount of active drug content as the reference product.[1] This article discusses challenges in reconciling this new thinking with the agency's stated views relative to biosimilar regulation and the generally accepted "totality of evidence" standard as discussed in the agency's guidance document, "Scientific Considerations in Demonstrating Biosimilarity to a Reference Product."[2] This contrast between strength, on the one hand, and potency (clinical function), on the other, is also important to consider relative to the implications of the intent of the Biologics Price Competition and Innovation Act of 2009 (BPCIA) — and how existing legislative ambiguities can be addressed and amended.

A Very Short History of the Biologics Price Competition and Innovation Act

The Biologics Price Competition and Innovation Act of 2009 (BPCIA) gave FDA authority to create a regulatory pathway for "biosimilar" biological products. The BPCIA amended the Public Health Service (PHS) Act to create an abbreviated approval pathway for biological products shown to be biosimilar to, or interchangeable with, an FDA-licensed reference biological product.

The development of this legislation included many different legislative iterations and scientific approaches. Two key issues, however, laid the groundwork for final passage: (1) that the intent of the legislation was to expedite the introduction of biosimilars into the US market in order to expand patient access to lower cost, safe, and effective biologics; and (2) to maintain FDA's regulatory flexibility in determining the scientific "rules of the road." As Dr. Jay Siegel (former Office Director, Office of Drug Evaluation Sciences at FDA) commented at a March 8, 2007, hearing of the Senate Health, Education, Labor and Pensions (HELP) Committee, "any proposed pathway should not constrain the FDA's ability to request data and studies in support of sound scientific decisions."[3]

While Congress creates statutory framework, it is often left to the regulatory agency (in this case, FDA) to further develop regulations and guidance. In the case of the BPCIA, the law lays out the intent but allows FDA to create both the ground rules and the guardrails. Such a flexible approach helps to empower the agency and stakeholders to develop creative, nimble, and dynamic regulatory approaches with which to build the global standards for innovative biosimilar regulatory science.

Congressional Intent vs. Regulatory Guidance

Biosimilars bring lower costs and greater access to the market for biological products, but FDA must determine a predictable pathway for development, review, and real-world use. The development of generic drugs — often cited as a model for biosimilars — actually illustrates the value of building a market step-by-step and taking a measured approach. Haste can waste breakthrough technology.

To make the biosimilars market a success in a reasonable timeframe, it is important to ensure that the regulatory process for biosimilars is one that instills confidence. Speeding products to market for commercial reasons without considering the appropriate required regulatory science can have just the opposite effect. A drive toward quality is typically reflected in FDA's deliberative approach and is a shared objective of stakeholders. Quality is in the agency's DNA. Prescribers want to know that the switching of biological products is supported by solid evidence and reflects the real world in which patients are likely to be switched by their insurers. Confidence will come largely through a judicious regulatory mix of creativity and predictability.[4] Regulatory predictability is the critical element in driving investment, without which there will be no biosimilars to consider. As FDA has made clear, confusion can lead to decreased confidence in the safety and effectiveness of agency-approved biosimilars for providers and patients.[5]

But what happens when regulatory ambiguity exists in the application of the underlying science — perhaps in ways Congress had not considered? This is precisely the situation regarding FDA guidance regarding a biosimilar's strength versus its potency. Not addressing this conflict may have potential unintended consequences of disincentivizing both the development and uptake of biosimilars. This is more than a rhetorical flourish. It is a distinction with a difference.

"Strength" vs. "Potency"

The debate is highlighted by industry's recent submission of a Citizen Petition,[6] requesting the Food and Drug Administration to make strength determinations for parenteral biologics based upon the total drug content of the container "without regard to concentration." Let's examine the argument.

The petition asserts that FDA's current interpretation of "strength" conflicts with the express terms and purpose of the BPCIA. Specifically, the petition observes that FDA has adopted a final policy that the "strength" of an injectable biological product (i.e., parenteral solution) is based on both the total content of drug substance (in mass or units of activity) and the concentration of drug substance (in mass or units of activity per unit volume). The assertion is made that FDA's current position changes the "same strength" requirement in section 351(k) of the PHS Act ("strength" defined as total drug content in the drug container regardless of concentration or total volume) to a new standard. Current guidance calls for a biological product approved under the 351(k) pathway to have the same concentration of drug substance as the reference product (RP), not just the same total drug content.

Per FDA's 2011 Guidance for Industry, "potency" is defined as "the specific ability or capacity of the product, as indicated by appropriate laboratory tests or by adequately controlled clinical data obtained through the administration of the product in the manner intended, to effect a given result." "Strength" is defined as "[t]he potency, that is, the therapeutic activity of the drug product as indicated by appropriate laboratory tests or by adequately developed and controlled clinical data."[7]

There is power in regulatory precedent. In FDA's existing guidance to industry,[8] the agency gives an overview of its approach to determining biosimilarity and discusses important scientific considerations in demonstrating biosimilarity, including:

- A stepwise approach to demonstrating biosimilarity, which can include a comparison of the proposed product and the reference product with respect to structure, function, animal toxicity, human pharmacokinetics (PK) and pharmacodynamics (PD), clinical immunogenicity, and clinical safety and effectiveness
- The totality-of-the-evidence approach that FDA will use to review applications for biosimilar products, consistent with a longstanding Agency approach to evaluation of scientific evidence
- General scientific principles in conducting comparative structural analyses, functional assays, animal testing, human PK and PD studies, clinical immunogenicity assessments, and comparative clinical studies (including clinical study design issues).

In the context of biosimilar regulation, "totality of evidence" means that sufficient structural, functional, nonclinical, and clinical data are acquired in a stepwise manner, to demonstrate that no clinically meaningful differences in quality, safety, or efficacy are observed compared with the reference product.[9]

Section 351(i) of the PHS Act defines biosimilarity to mean "that the biological product is highly similar to the reference product notwithstanding minor differences in clinically inactive components" and that "there are no clinically meaningful differences between the biological product and the reference product in terms of the safety, purity, and potency of the product."[10]

The petitioners urge the agency to alter its interpretation of the word "strength" found in the language of the BPCIA. At issue is an agency requirement that a biosimilar medicine must be the same strength as the brand-name biologic treatment. The petitioners argue that FDA's definition of strength is too restrictive because the agency requires a biosimilar to have the same total concentration of the active ingredient found in the injectable originator biologic, not just the total drug content, even if both treatments have the same clinical effect on patients.

From a regulatory science perspective (per the Citizen Petition), strength and concentration "had distinct, non-overlapping meanings when the BPCIA was enacted. And Congress omitted the term concentration from the BPCIA. The FDA's current interpretation of strength to include concentration, therefore conflicts" with the language found in the BPCIA.

One way to resolve this debate would be to amend the definition of "strength" (in reference to a biological product intended for administration by injection) to mean the total content of drug substance in the dosage form without regard to the concentration of drug substance or total volume of the biological product.[11]

Left unamended, the current regulatory situation presents ambiguities that may hamper innovation — a sizable roadblock to the intent of the BPCIA. If an innovator biologics manufacturer wins FDA approval for a new formulation of an existing treatment with a different dosage and concentration, a rival manufacturer would likely be told its product is only considered to be a biosimilar version of the older formulation, "similar" in strength but not "potency" to the newer formulation. This ultimately disadvantages healthcare professionals and patients. It isn't a message of "similarity" or therapeutic parity. But should we trade either for the value of incremental innovation? We must always be wary of a regulatory Hobson's Choice[12] between similarity and therapeutic parity.

The Citizen Petition's policy argument is that FDA's interpretation of the language in the BPCIA could make it rather easy for brand-name biologic manufacturers to introduce new formulations of existing treatments in order to thwart would-be biosimilar rivals from gaining a larger share of the market — a marked departure from the intent of the legislation. Per the Citizen Petition, "FDA's interpretation is unreasonable because it encourages, or at least permits, brand sponsors to use minor concentration changes as an anti-competitive tactic to prevent competition from biosimilar and interchangeable biosimilar products, thereby depriving patients from accessing more affordable biological products."

Per an article in the industry watch-dog publication STAT, "Consequently, the drug maker argued that the current FDA definition of the word 'strength' could make it impossible for certain products to win regulatory designation as a biosimilar or an interchangeable version of a newer formulation. In FDA parlance, interchangeable refers to the ability to substitute a biosimilar for a biologic without seeking permission from the prescribing health care provider."[13]

According to the Citizen Petition, "[T]his interpretation of 'strength' is incorrect as a matter of both law and policy. First, it conflicts with the clear meaning of 'strength' — an unambiguous term of art — which Congress adopted when it passed the BPCIA in 2009. Second, FDA's interpretation is unreasonable because it encourages, or at least permits, brand sponsors to use minor concentration changes as an anti-competitive tactic to prevent competition from biosimilar and interchangeable biosimilar products, thereby depriving patients from accessing more affordable biological products, contrary to the goals of the BPCIA.... FDA should still exercise discretion to change its policy because that definition better promotes the goals of the BPCIA, and there are no countervailing regulatory interests that outweigh this important benefit."[14]

One intent of the BPCIA was to allow FDA significant latitude in determining the scientific requirements for biosimilar development and regulatory review. But what happens when there is a perception that the agency's best scientific judgment comes into direct conflict with legislative intent?

Making BPCIA Better

No legislation, no matter how well-meaning, well-researched, argued, or written is ever perfect as first adopted. This is especially true for cutting-edge scientific issues — such as the regulation of biosimilars. That is why Congress regularly amends already-enacted legislation — to make our laws better and more in line with the original intent of Congress — and the evolving realities of regulatory science.

Consider the Drug Price Competition and Patent Term Restoration Act.[15] This historic healthcare legislation established a modern, fair, and feasible approval pathway for generic drug products, under which applicants can submit an abbreviated new drug application (ANDA) under section 505(j) of the Federal Food, Drug, and Cosmetic Act (FD&C Act). The intent of this landmark law was to both recognize and reward the importance of innovator investment but also to expedite (after a specific period of exclusivity) the introduction of safe and effective generic drugs in order to provide broader access to less expensive medicines. As revolutionary and impactful as this law was at the time, it was found to have some unintended consequences that needed to be addressed once it was in place. And this is precisely what happened. The Medicare Modernization Act of 2003 [16] (MMA) closed many of the same loopholes for generic drugs that the Citizen Petition argues to be contrary to the intent of the BPCIA's intent on biosimilars, specifically, allowing "evergreening" patents to slow free and fair marketplace competition.[17]

Pharmaceutical company rebates to pharmacy benefit managers (PBMs) that are tied to formulary restrictions create an incentive for entrenched market leaders to "bid" incremental rebates to prevent or limit access to competitive medicines. This model, coupled with escalating cost-sharing requirements, harms patients by driving up prices, which results in reducing access to innovative drugs.

There are many roadblocks preventing a more rapid penetration of biosimilars into the US market that are outside of the purview of the Food and Drug Administration. One such impediment is "exclusionary contracting."[18] When a group of pharmaceutical CEOs testified before the Senate Finance Committee in February 2019, Pfizer CEO Albert Bourla said he supported "reforms that would create a system in which transparent, upfront discounts benefit patients at the pharmacy counter, rather than a system driven by rebates that are swallowed up by companies up and down the supply chain."[19] When asked if they would lower prices if PBMs played fair, every hand on the panel went up.[20]

This is not an academic exercise. Although biologics only account for 2 percent of all prescriptions written in the US, they are responsible for $120 billion or 37 percent of net drug spending and, since 2014, for 93 percent of the overall growth in total spending.[21] If we don't reflect on the important policy implications of questions such as "strength vs. potency," we face the very possibility of not being able to pay for new innovation to problems ranging from Alzheimer's disease to pandemic therapeutics and vaccines.

We must continue to work toward a healthcare ecosystem based on competitive, predictable, free-market principles while embracing the best, most current thinking in regulatory science. Thoughtful members of the healthcare ecosystem can disagree on issues such as "strength vs. potency." But we must all be cognizant of the bigger picture — that of providing broader access to safe and effective medicines, be they generic drugs or biosimilars. If we fail to embrace this shared mission, we do a tremendous disservice to advancing the value and accessibility of healthcare in America.

"We are our choices." - Jean-Paul Sartre

REFERENCES

1. https://www.fda.gov/drugs/biosimilars/biosimilar-and-interchangeable-products#reference.

2. https://www.fda.gov/media/82647/download.

3. https://www.help.senate.gov/hearings/follow-on-biologics; Note: At the time of this hearing, Dr. Siegel was an employee of Johnson & Johnson.

4. https://www.healthaffairs.org/do/10.1377/hblog20180904.284795/full/.

5. https://www.fda.gov/media/150751/download.

6. https://www.accessdata.fda.gov/scripts/cdrh/cfdocs/cfcfr/CFRSearch.cfm?FR=10.30.

7. https://www.fda.gov/media/79856/download.

8. https://www.fda.gov/media/82647/download.

9. https://www.ncbi.nlm.nih.gov/pmc/articles/PMC6566480/.

10. Section 7002(b)(3) of the Affordable Care Act, adding section 351(i)(2) of the PHS Act.

11. In fact, an amendment to Representative Scott Peters' healthcare bill reads:

12. SEC. 208. CHANGE IN DEFINITION OF STRENGTH FOR THE PURPOSES OF DETERMINING INTERCHANGEABILITY OF BIOLOGICAL AND BIOSIMILAR PRODUCTS. (a) Section 351(i) of the Public Health Service Act is amended by inserting the following: The term "strength," in reference to a biological product intended for administration by injection, means the total content of drug substance in the dosage form without regard to the concentration of drug substance or total volume of the biological product. (b) Section 351(k)(7)(C)(ii)(I) of the Public Health Service Act is amended by inserting "concentration," after "delivery device."

13. https://en.wikipedia.org/wiki/Hobson.

14. https://en.wikipedia.org/wiki/Hobson%27s_choice.

15. https://www.statnews.com/pharmalot/2020/12/10/boehringer-fda-biosimilar-biologic-petition/.

16. https://www.boehringer-ingelheim.us/sites/us/files/files/boehringer-ingelheim-bpcia-strength-petition.pdf.

17. https://en.wikipedia.org/wiki/Drug_Price_Competition_and_Patent_Term_Restoration_Act.

18. https://www.congress.gov/bill/108th-congress/house-bill/1.

19. https://academic.oup.com/jlb/article/5/3/590/5232981.

20. https://biosimilarscouncil.org/wp-content/uploads/2019/04/Breaking-Through-on-Biosimilars-Biosimilars-Council-White-Paper.pdf.

21. https://www.finance.senate.gov/hearings/drug-pricing-in-america-a-prescription-for-change-part-ii.

22. https://www.statnews.com/2019/07/11/drug-rebates-white-house-decision/.

23. https://jamanetwork.com/journals/jamanetworkopen/fullarticle/2764808#:~:text=Although%20biologics%20only%20account%20for,overall%20growth%20in%20total%20spending.

The Major Healthcare and Cybersecurity Risk of "-to-Repair" Laws

By Peter J. Pitts

Originally published in *The Hill*, June 29, 2021

Just like other devices we rely on, medical devices can improve our quality of life — so long as they are maintained to work properly. When they are not — or not maintained or serviced in line with FDA approval — there can be huge healthcare and cybersecurity risks.

In the brief on a just-released FDA discussion paper, William Maisel notes, "Many medical devices are reusable and need preventative maintenance and repair during their useful life; therefore, proper servicing is critical to their continued safe and effective use." Maisel, M.D., is the director of the Office of Product Evaluation and Quality in FDA's Center for Devices and Radiological Health. Who could possibly disagree with such a statement? Lawyers.

That's right, the tort bar is prioritizing profit over patient safety. For shame. (No, I'm not surprised either.)

Quality is the glue that holds together our healthcare technology ecosystem. Whether it's a medicine for high blood pressure, a COVID-19 vaccine, or a medical device such as an implantable stent or a room-size MRI machine, the FDA's mission rests upon a triad of trust — safety, effectiveness, and quality. And the bedrock upon which quality rests is Good Manufacturing Practices. Who could be against that? Lawyers.

Consider the recent spate of suggested state and federal legislation on what is called "Right-to-Repair." At first glance, it seems like a good idea. Why not make it easier for consumers to fix their broken electronics, without having to pay a costly sum to the original manufacturer? But, as HL Mencken reminds us, "for every complex problem there is an answer that is clear, simple, and wrong." The reality is that Right-to-Repair presents many dangerous unintended consequences. The No.1 problem is that it compromises patient safety.

The core of Right-to-Repair laws is to require innovative technology companies to make product repair information, replacement parts, and tools readily available to consumers and third-party repair shops. Should that be the case for devices such as Automated External Defibrillators and hospital ventilators? What about electrocardiograph (ECG) machines? Can physicians and patients be confident in non-FDA compliant vendors without the advanced training and technical ability to properly repair and recalibrate lifesaving machines? Who could argue that "anyone can do it?" Lawyers.

Why? Because when things go wrong, when medical devices fail, when patients and their families suffer the consequences, when associated healthcare costs skyrocket — it seems lawyers see opportunity. And they aim their lightening lances of litigation at the deepest pockets — the original manufacturers.

It seems the tort bar is creating a problem they can exploit for profit.

But wait, it gets worse. By allowing third parties without any FDA competence to repair regulated, complicated medical devices, Right-to-Repair also opens the door to breaches in cybersecurity.

According to the FDA, "cybersecurity is a widespread issue affecting medical devices connected to the Internet, networks, and other devices. Cybersecurity is the process of preventing unauthorized access, modification, misuse or denial of use, or the unauthorized use of information that is stored, accessed, or transferred from a medical device to an external recipient."

In the just-released FDA discussion paper that I referenced above, "Strengthening Cybersecurity Practices Associated with Servicing Medical Devices: Challenges and Opportunities," the agency asks, "How can entities that service medical devices contribute to strengthening the cybersecurity of medical devices?"

According to the discussion paper, "FDA defines service to be the repair and/or preventive or routine maintenance of one or more parts in a finished device, after distribution, for purposes of returning it to the safety and performance specifications established by the original equipment manufacturer (OEM) and to meet its original intended use."

In other words, the first step in advancing medical device cybersecurity is to limit and ensure that those who control repairs and maintenance of these highly sophisticated pieces of healthcare technology are regulated FDA manufacturers.

On July 27, the FDA is holding a public meeting on this topic. It couldn't be timelier. The proper servicing and security of medical devices and other healthcare technologies mustn't be subsumed for profit.

Counterfeit Drugs in a Post-Pandemic World

When asked why he robbed banks, the Depression-era folk hero Willie Sutton answered, "Because that's where the money is."

Just as COVID-19 mutates to survive and thrive, so too do the purveyors of counterfeit medicines. These false prophets of false profits use, as their high-speed host, the digitization of patient care. The future is now. So, how do we balance moving forward with user-friendly digitization, telemedicine, and virtual healthcare delivery while simultaneously recognizing the unintended consequences of the innovative criminal mind? The first step is to recognize there's a problem.

The Spreading Cancer of Counterfeit Drugs

By Peter J. Pitts

Originally published in the *Journal of Commercial Biotechnology*, October 29, 2020

Introduction

Just as the coronavirus mutates to survive and thrive, so to do the purveyors of counterfeit medicines — with their high-speed "host" being the digitization of patient care. The future is now. So, how do we balance moving forward with user-friendly digitization, telemedicine, and virtual healthcare delivery while simultaneously recognizing the unintended consequences of the innovative criminal mind? The first step is to recognize there's a problem.

Counterfeit Medicines: A Moveable Feast

Once upon a time, at the beginning of the new millennium, counterfeit medicines in the United States were largely "lifestyle" products such as erectile dysfunction drugs — Viagra being the poster child of the problem.[1] Other categories of fake pills included treatments for depression.[2] The common denominator was patient shame and embarrassment. Ordering from seemingly benign (i.e., "from Canada") websites seemed like a safe and anonymous way to address their conditions without having to visit either a physician, mental health professional, or pharmacist. A second category of counterfeit prey were people seeking higher-risk drugs (opioids, steroids, etc.) to facilitate a more dangerous lifestyle. The rationale for this second group was easier access to more dangerous (often controlled) substances.[3]

To respond to this emerging threat, the FDA formed a Counterfeit Drug Task Force in July 2003.[4] As a former FDA Associate Commissioner, I was proud to serve as a member of that task force. We received extensive comment from security experts, federal and state law enforcement officials, technology developers, manufacturers, wholesalers, retailers, consumer groups, and the general public on a very broad range of ideas for deterring counterfeiters. Those comments reinforced the need for the FDA to take action in multiple areas to create a comprehensive system of modern protections against counterfeit drugs.

At the FDA we discussed those ideas and developed a framework for a 21st-century pharmaceutical supply chain that would be more secure against modern counterfeit threats. The specific approach to assuring that Americans are protected from counterfeit drugs includes the following eight elements:

1. Implementation of new technologies to better protect our drug supply.
2. Adoption of electronic track and trace technology.

3. Adoption and enforcement of strong, proven anticounterfeiting laws and regulations by individual US states.
4. Increased criminal penalties to deter counterfeiting and more adequately punish those convicted.
5. Adoption of secure business practices by all participants in the drug supply chain.
6. Development of a system that helps ensure effective reporting of counterfeit drugs to the FDA and which strengthens the agency's rapid response to such reports.
7. Education of consumers and health professionals about the risks of counterfeit drugs and how to protect against them.
8. Collaboration with foreign stakeholders to develop strategies to deter and detect counterfeit drugs globally.

According to that report, "Although the safety and security of the US pharmaceutical supply is high, FDA's investigations show that counterfeiting of legitimate drug products poses a significant and growing problem. A multi-prong anti-counterfeiting strategy is necessary to protect consumers by preventing the introduction of counterfeit drugs, facilitating the introduction of counterfeit drugs, and minimizing the risk and exposure of consumers to counterfeit drugs."[5]

Congress also stepped in with legislation, including the Drug Safety and Accountability Act of 2010 and the FDA Globalization Act.[6]

The FDA adopted a global strategy for assuring the safety of the US supply chain that included creation of an office to oversee import safety, with stepped-up powers to interdict incoming drug shipments into the United States, collaborate with regulatory agencies in other countries, and order recalls of unsafe products. The agency also called on manufacturers to improve their own screenings of raw materials produced outside the United States — and began ranking more than 1,000 active drug ingredients to assess their "respective risk of economically motivated adulteration," according to then FDA Commissioner Dr. Margaret Hamburg.[7]

In a 2011 analysis of 8,000 rogue websites, the National Association of Boards of Pharmacy concluded that 96 percent of them were out of compliance with US pharmacy laws, and 85 percent didn't require a valid prescription.[8]

The FDA required legal distributors to keep detailed records of the sources of the medications they dispense.[9] But it proved to be a futile undertaking swiftly overtaken by advancing digital technologies and criminal talent. Drug counterfeiters have become so sophisticated, they can produce both drugs and packaging that cannot be differentiated from the real thing without complex, time-consuming, and costly analyses. It became quickly obvious that paper "pedigrees" were next to useless — but no new strategies, tactics were forthcoming from the FDA and Congress granted the agency neither additional funding nor enhanced regulatory powers to more robustly fight medicines counterfeiting. In 2004, when the FDA claimed that counterfeit drugs were being used to fund global terrorism,[10] many high-profile elected officials accused the agency of being in the pocket of Big Pharma. Today, these same politicians are strangely silent.

Sixteen years later the problem of counterfeit medicines is only getting worse.

Counterfeits Advance from Lifestyle to Lifesaving Drugs

When asked why he robbed banks, the Depression-era folk hero Willie Sutton answered, "Because that's where the money is."[11] That same dynamic explains why drug counterfeiters have changed their focus from lifestyle medicines to lifesaving/extending treatments — particularly oncology treatments (both oral and biological). It's where the money is. Fakes are almost impossible to identify without a sophisticated knowledge of packaging tools and techniques (see Appendix A). The digitization of healthcare has acted as an accelerant to the increased prevalence of and negative impact of counterfeit medicines.

This new and nefarious sales and marketing strategy may be good for the criminal bottom line — but it's deadly for patients.

The FDA has always battled to, on the one hand, empower patients while, on the other, protecting the public from incorrect, exaggerated, and downright phony health information and products. For the FDA, regulatory enforcement surrounding the proliferation of dietary supplements, cannabis, and cannabidiol (CBD) products have, at least to-date, been the battleground.[12] Today the issue is the same — a lack of resources and authority to adequately fight multiple battles simultaneously, but the stakes are higher.

According to a recent FDA statement:

> FDA lab tests have confirmed that at least one batch of a counterfeit version of Roche's Altuzan distributed in the United States contains no active ingredient. Even if the identified product were not counterfeit, Altuzan (bevacizumab), an injectable cancer medicine, is not approved by FDA for sale in the United States. The only FDA-approved version of bevacizumab for sale in the United States is called Avastin, marketed by Genentech.[13]

On July 17, 2020, the US Department of Justice announced the arrest of two men from Ukraine who admitted in federal court that they conspired to smuggle and distribute counterfeit cancer and hepatitis C drugs into the United States.[14] The DOJ reports that Maksym Nienadov, the owner of the Ukrainian-based company Healthy Nation, and his co-conspirator and employee — Volodymyr Nikolaienko — pleaded guilty in federal court in Houston, Texas, to conspiracy, trafficking in counterfeit drugs, and smuggling goods into the United States. Nienadov also admitted to introducing misbranded drugs into the United States. The investigation was conducted by Immigration and Customs Enforcement's Homeland Security Investigations and FDA's Office of Criminal Investigations.

The same problem exists in Canada and Europe. The World Health Organization recently warned cancer patients in North America and Europe about a batch of fake drugs that contain nothing but a common painkiller. The product alert says that counterfeit medicine packaged to look like the cancer drug Iclusig, known generically as ponatinib — a targeted therapy for chronic myeloid and acute lymphoblastic leukemia — simply contains acetaminophen.[14] The fakes, discovered by a Swiss wholesaler, have also been detected in Turkey and Argentina.[15]

A weeklong, Interpol-coordinated blitz saw authorities in 116 countries seize 500 tons of fake pharmaceuticals worth an estimated $14.000.000. The haul included anti-inflammatory medication, birth control pills, and counterfeit treatments for HIV, Parkinson's, and diabetes (Investigators also found more than 110,000 fake medical devices like hearing aids, contact lenses, and syringes). The seizures resulted in 859 arrests and the closure of 3,671 weblinks.[16]

Rather than attracting otherwise healthy people looking for a quick and private way to purchase low-cost Viagra (out of their own pockets), today's victims are desperately ill patients looking for a way to afford their medicines in the face of rising and perpetual insurance co-payments.[17] The unintended consequences of pharmacy benefit manager (PBM) tactics such as copay accumulators and maximizers[18] as well as federal government regulations that preclude the use of many patient assistance programs[19] have left patients with cancer and other life-threatening diseases looking for an alternative route to access. Prescription drug counterfeiters have recognized the opportunity and rushed into the breach.[20] Nature abhors a vacuum.

The Role of Specialty Pharmacy
What has made this possible and predictable is the rapid rise of "Specialty Pharmacy." Specialty pharmacy refers to distribution channels designed to handle pharmaceutical therapies that are either high cost, high complexity, and/or high touch (products that require a much higher degree of personal attention and service). Specialty pharmacy requires a higher degree of complexity in terms of distribution, administration, and patient management, which drives up the cost of the drugs.[21]

Initially specialty pharmacy providers attached "high-touch services to their overall price tags" arguing that patients who receive specialty pharmaceuticals "need high levels of ancillary and follow-up care to ensure that the drug spend is not wasted on them." In the mid-1990s, there were fewer than 30 specialty drugs on the market; by 2008 that number had increased to 200 [22] and by 2018 more than 900 unique pharmacy locations received specialty pharmacy accreditation — a 25 percent increase from 2017.[23]

Importantly, the pharmaceutical industry, in close collaboration with specialty pharmacy, actively and aggressively drove online service and mail-order delivery. Why is specialty pharmacy relevant to the issue of the evolution of counterfeiting? Opportunity.

Specialty pharmacy creates a powerful "cover story" for criminal counterfeiters. Legitimate insurance companies and PBMs are delivering legitimate medicines through the US Postal Service, creating a false sense of security for patients. Two of the serious unintended consequences of using the US Mail are quality and timing problems (see below). Since patients are regularly receiving their medicines through the mail and experience the legitimate system's lack of precision, patients accept the legitimacy of the process. As a result, patients lower their guard and open the door for all types of pharmaceutical interactions that occur virtually or through mail. This creates a dangerous and brightly lit opportunity for counterfeiters to "impersonate" specialty pharmacy and insert counterfeit medicines, via the US Postal Service, into the medicine chests of desperately ill patients. This is the same pathway of opportunity counterfeiters follow when they place a Canadian flag on their phony websites that promise "FDA-Approved Drugs at Canadian prices." (The issue of drug importation will be addressed later in this report.)

While mailing a prescription may sound routine, many of the patients forced to wait for these services are those with complex or life-threatening conditions such as cancer. Delaying these treatments can have serious repercussions for these patients' health and potentially lessens their outlook.

A report from the *Columbus Dispatch* in 2018 highlighted the problem, finding patients like Elvin Weir who not only had to wait for his prescription to be sent to him, but he was also sent the incorrect medication twice. PBMs and insurers claim that specialty pharmacies help to manage care and costs, but in Mr. Weir's case, their "care" led to a delay in his treatment and the waste of $20,000 worth of treatments.[24]

Another 2018 report from the *Times-Picayune* in New Orleans highlighted how numerous cancer patients are forced to wait or are outright denied the medication their doctor has prescribed them, forcing them to wait for an appeal. In the instance highlighted, the patient, Connie Raborn, had to wait almost three months before she was able to take her medication.[25] Such delays aren't the only problems facing patients using a specialty or mail-order pharmacy. Patients have reported receiving medications that were shipped at unsafe temperatures, rendering them ineffective or even dangerous.[26] It is a short step from substandard medicines to counterfeit ones.

The Regulatory Limitations of Product Serialization

Serialization refers to the requirements for application of a unique identification code, a serial Number, or electronic product code (EPC). Serial numbers can be tracked through its entire supply chain, from production to retail distribution to final dispensation to the patient.[27]

The FDA believes that counterfeiting can be reduced significantly through product serialization. Serialization requires a comprehensive system to track and trace the passage of prescription drugs through the entire supply chain. Serialization can potentially identify every product by a unique serial number in addition to the origin, shelf life and batch number for that product. This could potentially allow the product's lifecycle to be traced from production, through distribution, and finally to the patient. But serialization is not just about generating unique serial numbers, but also creating and maintaining identification tools that provide visibility and full traceability within the supply chain. It requires collaborative action from partners throughout the supply chain for accurate recording, tracking, and managing of data as the product moves from manufacturer, to distributor, to the dispensing point. It's expensive and a complex proposition. That complexity creates a multitude of opportunities for criminal counterfeiters motivated by huge profits on placing their fake products into the medicine chests of American patients.

The Drug Quality and Security Act

As part of a long-term strategy, the United States has been trying to move to implementing technology and systems that would discourage the introduction and distribution of counterfeit drugs. In November 2013, President Obama signed into law the Drug Quality and Security Act (DQSA) (H.R. 3204).[28] Implicit within the DSQA is the Drug Supply Chain Security Act (DSCSA), which outlines critical steps to build an electronic, interoperable system to identify and trace certain prescription drugs as they are distributed in the US. This law established requirements to facilitate the tracing of prescription drug products through the pharmaceutical supply distribution chain (H.R.3204 — Drug Quality and Security Act, 2018).[29]

Full execution of Title II of the DQSA[30] dictates that data will be exchanged across a very complex and diverse set of supply chain partners: in-house packaging facilities, packaging facilities of contract development and manufacturing organizations (CDMOs), third-party logistics providers (3PLs), repackagers, wholesalers, and dispensers. However, the aggregation of serialized data is not a requirement of the DQSA.

Data must have high integrity and be free of corruption for effective use by members of the pharmaceutical supply chain, and data must be protected from hackers and other cyber criminals. Serialization is, of course, meant to protect and validate the identity of a product throughout the supply chain. Therefore, it does not take much of a leap of imagination to envision how cybercounterfeiters benefit by manipulating the identity of high-value products — at the expense of patients seeking lower costs due to ever-increasing co-payments driven by the costs of specialty pharmacy and the desire of PBMs to further increase their bottom-line profits.[31]

Theoretically, by the end of 2023 (the deadline for full track-and-trace implementation) an enormous amount of data will be generated at operational speeds, correctly assigned to a given product, stored, and transmitted to all appropriate supply chain partners. That data will then need to flow seamlessly between clients and their Contract Development and Manufacturing Organization (CDMO) or Contract Packaging Organization (CPO).[32] Theoretically. However, as the biopharmaceutical industry, its supply chain partners, PBMs (and their specialty pharmacy divisions), regulators, and lawmakers continue to discuss, debate, and finesse serialization in all its forms, criminal counterfeiters are exploiting the holes in the system, enhancing their false profits through savvy exploitation of technology and regulatory gaps — at the expense of patient health.

HHS Office of Inspector General Report: The Drug Supply Chain Security Act (DSCSA)

In February 2020, the US Department of Health and Human Services Office of Inspector General issued a report[33] that stated:

> Drug diversion, counterfeiting, and the importation of unapproved drugs may result in potentially dangerous drugs entering the drug supply chain, posing a threat to public health and safety. To enhance the security of this supply chain, the DSCSA requires trading partners in the drug supply chain to create a record of each drug product transaction. FDA can use these records to investigate and identify potentially harmful drug products, prevent further distribution, and facilitate efficient recalls.

According to the report, ownership of 37 of 44 selected drug products could be traced through the supply chain using drug product tracing information that the Drug Supply Chain Security Act (DSCSA) requires. Seven selected drug products could not be completely traced to manufacturers. Typically, this was because tracing documents exchanged between the wholesale distributor and manufacturer were missing or had mismatched tracing information.

In one instance, a wholesale distributor refused to provide tracing documents. When tracing information is missing or mismatched, a complete tracing record for a drug product may not always be available to support investigations of suspect or illegitimate drug products in the supply chain, which could delay investigators. Indeed, staff at the Food and Drug Administration (FDA) reported that accurate tracing information is critical to identifying a drug product quickly in the event of a recall or when removing an illegitimate drug product from the supply chain.

Additionally, for 21 of 44 selected drug products, the Inspector General found that — unlike with their ownership — they could not trace their physical movement through the supply chain using tracing information. Nor could the OIG identify the shipping locations of trading partners (e.g., manufacturers, wholesale distributors, and dispensers) or third-party logistics providers that shipped or stored the drugs on behalf of the trading partners. Although the DSCSA does not require this information, should FDA not have access to this information in case of a drug safety emergency, FDA and other investigators would need to request additional documents, which could delay investigations and hamper FDA's ability to identify sources of potentially harmful drugs in a timely manner.

The OIG report recommends that FDA follow up with the wholesale distributor that did not provide tracing information. The OIG also recommends that FDA offer educational outreach to trading partners about required drug product tracing information and data standardization guidelines. Lastly, the OIG recommends that FDA seek legislative authority to require information about a drug product's complete physical path through the supply chain on tracing information. FDA concurred with all of the OIG report recommendations.

Bad Policy Ideas Have Negative Real-World Consequences

We live in a hyper-politicized environment often driven by simplistic, sound-bite solutions to complex problems — such as the cost of medicines. In the case of counterfeit medicines, they can actually exacerbate the problem. A good example of this issue is Drug Importation (aka: "Drugs from Canada").

The concept sounds easy and logical but, as HL Mencken said, "For every complex problem there is an answer that is clear, simple, and wrong." All importation schemes offer lower-cost medicines with no additional risk. The facts, however, point to neither savings — nor safety.

During a weeklong anti-counterfeiting operation Canadian officials inspected nearly 3,600 packages — and found that 87 percent contained counterfeit or unlicensed health products.[34]

A striking number of "Canadian" drugs aren't actually from Canada. Canadian internet pharmacies regularly import drugs from less developed[35] and less regulated countries, like Turkey. Then they slap on their own labels and ship them elsewhere.[36] One FDA operation found 85 percent of "Canadian" drugs originated in 27 different countries and more than a third of those drugs were potentially counterfeit.[37]

Such concerns explain why Illinois ditched its importation program, I-SaveRX, in 2009 after failing to adequately inspect foreign pharmacies. According to a state audit, "40 percent of the required inspections of the foreign entities claiming to be pharmacies were never completed, putting patients at risk" and patients were left with "no regulator to protect them."[38]

Canadian regulators have warned Americans that importation could be risky. One official at Health Canada, the government agency that oversees that nation's pharmaceutical supply[39] said the regulator "does not assure that products being sold to US citizens are safe, effective and of high quality and does not intend to do so in the future."[40] Safety cannot be ignored because it is inconvenient.

Senior US officials have issued similar warnings. Over the past 18 years, in both Democrat and Republican administrations, every FDA commissioner and secretary of Health and Human Services has failed to certify that importation is safe.[41]

However, recently, The Department of Health and Human Services (HHS) recently floated a proposal, dubbed the Safe Importation Plan, to allow Americans to use Canada as their personal pharmacy.[42] In Canada, the government dictates the market through price controls, but any drug importation scheme should give Americans pause.[43]

The so-called Safe Importation Action Plan offers two paths forward for drug importation. First, states, wholesalers, or pharmacists could submit plans for demonstration projects for HHS to review outlining how they would import Health Canada-approved drugs. Second, manufacturers could import versions of existing FDA-approved drugs into the United States.

The plan sounds reasonable enough, but it's missing one key variable — the Canadian government. Neither the Trump Administration nor any state that's been pondering drug importation has ever consulted the Canadian government.[44] Had they done so, they'd see that our neighbors to the north have some serious concerns with the proposal.

Access to high-quality medicines is a crucial issue, but drug importation is not the answer. The Trump Administration's drug importation plan would create more problems than it would solve by jeopardizing Canada's drug supply and exposing Americans to deadly counterfeits.

The CDC and the "Epidemiology of Counterfeiting"

Through literature review, interviews, surveillance, and research, discover new data about counterfeiting as a risk to public health. With a lack of information on the public safety impact on the most at-risk populations (economically disadvantaged, elderly, underinsured), the Centers for Disease Control and Prevention (CDC) should develop and field a study on the adverse health effects of counterfeit medicines. The scope of such a project should include:

- Raising awareness of counterfeit medicines as a public health issue within CDC and among its partners.
- In-depth interviews to determine which CDC programs and partners use prescription drugs in prevention, intervention, treatment, and surveillance programs, identify baseline awareness of counterfeit medicine within the same groups.
- A literature review to determine if there is existing evidence of counterfeit medicines in the peer-reviewed literature, assess the current landscape (and associated consumer harms) and identify gaps and areas for future research.
- Collect data and determine commonalities of counterfeit-related injuries, disease, identify determinants and identify further areas for prevention.
- Develop a report to summarize key findings and recommendations, including potential subject matter experts, opportunities for further collaboration, and development of a framework for additional phases of research.

Counterfeits and COVID: Problem and Opportunity

Not surprisingly, the COVID-19 pandemic has increased the public's exposure to counterfeit medical products.

According to the FDA:

> The FDA advises consumers to be cautious of websites and stores selling products that claim to prevent, treat or cure COVID-19. There are no FDA-approved products to prevent COVID-19. Products marketed for veterinary use, or "for research use only," or otherwise not for human consumption, have not been evaluated for safety and should

never be used by humans. For example, the FDA is aware of people trying to prevent COVID-19 by taking a product called chloroquine phosphate, which is sold to treat parasites in aquarium fish. Products for veterinary use or for "research use only" may have adverse effects, including serious illness and death, when taken by people. Don't take any form of chloroquine unless it has been prescribed for you by your health care provider and obtained from legitimate sources.

The sale of fraudulent COVID-19 products is a threat to the public health. If you are concerned about the spread of COVID-19, talk to your health care provider and follow the advice of FDA's federal partners.[45]

The FDA recognizes the threat of criminals preying on the COVID-19 fears of the American public. The agency acted quickly and aggressively issue warnings and ramp up enforcement. Perhaps, in a post-COVID environment, the FDA will pursue the threat of counterfeit medicines in a more proactive manner.

Reinforcing the Strongest Link in the Chain

The war against counterfeiting requires robust leadership and new strategies and tactics. The Center for Medicine in the Public Interest believes the FDA is the most appropriate federal authority to lead our nation's anti-counterfeiting efforts. And the first order of business is to create a task force that includes other entities from the US Department of Health and Human Services (National Institutes of Health, Centers for Disease Control), other cabinet-level departments (Justice, Commerce, Homeland Security, the White House, etc.), state-level authorities, and professional and patient organizations. You can't win a war without a war room. And you cannot fight battles without precise coordination of resources and effort.

The most potent tool in the struggle against counterfeiting is product integrity. Quality is hard to maintain, and counterfeiters don't care about it. That is their Achilles' heel. Advancing and protecting quality is the most powerful weapon in the fight counterfeit medicines.

Comprehensive product quality and supply-chain security requires a multilayer approach that includes prevention, detection, and response strategies and actions. The battle against counterfeit medicines requires a comprehensive resource that addresses areas of vulnerability in the medical product supply chain and contains recommended best practices and tools to prevent and detect substandard and falsified medical products before they reach consumers. Such a resource must also provide tools to efficiently and effectively respond to incidents involving substandard and falsified medical products.

Consider the FDA's Supply Chain Security Tool Kit announced earlier this year. The toolkit contains training materials intended to educate regulators, industry, healthcare professionals, and others on a particular part of the supply chain in 10 categories:

- Good manufacturing practices
- Good distribution practices
- Good import/export practices
- Clinical/retail pharmacy practices
- Product security
- Detection technology
- Internet sales
- Track and trace systems
- Surveillance and monitoring
- Single points of contact

According to the FDA, "The toolkit will be used by industry stakeholders and regulators from around the globe to adopt best practices, for training purposes, and to strengthen laws and regulations to protect consumers from unsafe and substandard drug products. APEC Training Centers of Excellence for Regulatory Science (CoE) will be established to further training and use of the toolkit."[46]

This is an important and timely effort and should be supported with more than just rhetoric. As we enter into PDUFA reauthorization discussions,[47] support of this initiative should be a priority.

But the FDA can do more. As the strongest link in the chain, the FDA must also be at the forefront of stronger criminal prosecution (in close collaboration with the Department of Justice), enhanced enforcement of dietary supplement health claims (together with the FCC and the Department of Commerce), targeted education efforts to oncology professionals (physicians, nurses, pharmacists), patients, caregivers, and payers (alongside the National Cancer Institute).

It is also important that the FDA not undermine its own efforts by "going soft" on ill-considered policies that support the importation of foreign prescription medicines (see above section, "Bad Policy Ideas Have Negative Real-World Consequences"). Just as the embrace of specialty pharmacy has created an opportunity for criminal counterfeiting, so too does the patina of FDA "approval" of the importation concept. It is essential that the FDA actively avoid allowing its own words to provide cover for those who would harm the public health for their own profit.

Friendly fire is often the most costly.

Moving Forward: 10 Steps to Victory

1. Increase awareness of counterfeit threat, particularly associated with life-extending/saving medicines, among patients and healthcare providers.
2. Differentiate target audiences. Demand reduction for patients/HCPs to prevent inadvertent purchase of suspect product. Partner with law enforcement to address willful violators.
3. Demand reduction must be measurable (per HHS/OIG report).
4. Create personal serialization validation tools to enable patient participation.
5. Conduct a CDC "Epidemiology of Counterfeit Medicines" study — how many patients actually die or are seriously harmed by counterfeit oncology medicines? Who are they?[48]
6. Enhance productive industry/government intelligence/information exchange.
7. Make better use of existing government resources and authorities for more effective protection of patients/citizens.
8. Enhance industry/government collaboration on demand reduction.
9. Eliminate use of the internet as a commercial platform by effectively educating and partnering with recalcitrant ISPs.[49]
10. Increase awareness programs for the general population of the problem and of programs that reduce co-payment costs.

Source: http://www.nifds.go.kr/apec/SupplyChain/APEC_SupplyChainToolkit_170317.pdf

Concluding Thoughts

The unfortunate reality is that urgent public health issues (such as COVID-19 and the danger of counterfeit drugs) that should be strictly nonpolitical are being seen, first and foremost, as opportunities by special interest groups and many of our elected representatives to "score points." The media, alas, swarms to cover these blood feuds, almost entirely obfuscating the scope and severity of the problem. When it comes to counterfeit drugs, the alarm bells sounded by the biopharmaceutical industry are too often waved off as an attempt to distract attention from "the high cost of drugs." While such exhortations are tactically successful in attracting transient media coverage, it does a tremendous disservice to the public by masking the urgency of the problem. As *Scientific American* reports, "In a fiercely competitive business. For those who like pharma scandals, their paper offers detailed examples, a la 'The Constant Gardener,' of pharmaceutical companies trying to bury their problems quietly."[50]

During my tenure on the FDA's Counterfeit Drug Task Force, I witnessed first-hand the evolution of thinking within the biopharmaceutical industry. Initially, as suggested by the *Scientific American* article, industry's response was to address the problem but say nothing publicly for fear of counterfeit drugs tainting their own reputation. When pressed by the FDA Task Force to take a more public leadership position, industry swiftly stepped up to the plate, partnering with the FDA and other government agencies (on both the federal and state levels) to more publicly and aggressively address the problems associated with mitigating and preventing the growth of counterfeit drugs in the United States. Per *Scientific American*, "Pharma shows increased recognition that openness to the problem and notification of the public is not only the appropriate response but will likely reduce their liability and is otherwise in their self-interest."[51]

According to the FDA Task Force's initial report, "Based on what it has heard to date, the Task Force believes that the most constructive approach to addressing the problem of counterfeit drugs lies in identifying vulnerabilities in the drug distribution system and addressing those vulnerabilities with a multi-pronged approach." It isn't the "cost of drugs" that drives desperately ill patients into the arms of counterfeiters, it is, in the majority, the cost of patient co-pays. Larger and larger co-pays and out-of-pocket costs magnify the problem by creating a criminal opportunity. Better, more targeted, and aggressive regulation together with more regular and robust law enforcement is key — but when patients cannot afford their co-pay for lifesaving medicines, the incentive for quick-fix solutions via a website that promises to provide the genuine article is almost irresistible. As the old Yiddish proverb reminds us, "Sometimes a bargain is too expensive." And sometimes It's deadly. The time is now. Action must be taken. Attention must be paid.

Appendix A
Examples of Counterfeit Biologics

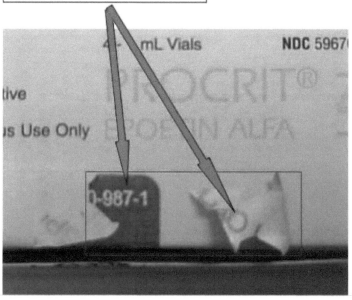

Authentic PROCRIT carton P004677 and
P007645. Carton closure seals are designed to
breakaway and leave a residue on the box
when removed. The words "OBPLP VOID" in
random order should appear on the underside
of the label or residue.

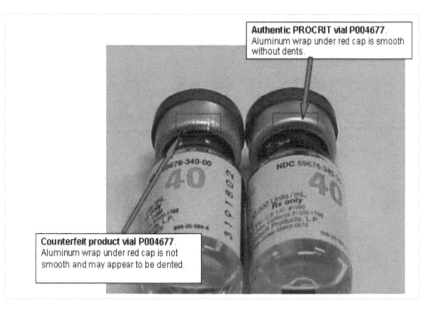

Authentic PROCRIT vial P004677.
Aluminum wrap under red cap is smooth
without dents.

Counterfeit product vial P004677.
Aluminum wrap under red cap is not
smooth and may appear to be dented.

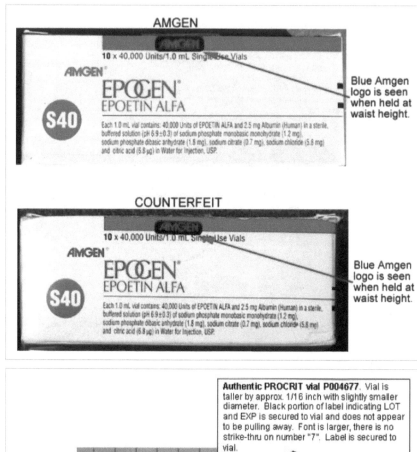

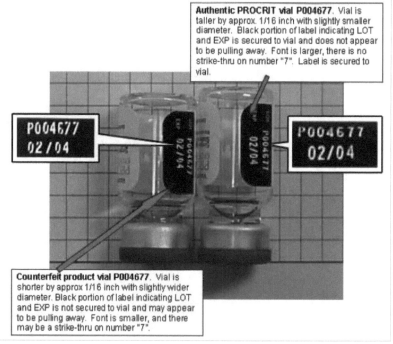

REFERENCES

1. https://www.pharmaceutical-technology.com/features/featuretackling-counterfeit-viagra-4970635/. Last accessed June 4, 2020.

2. https://www.cnbc.com/2018/08/02/antianxiety-drugs-fuel-the-next-deadly-drug-crisis-in-us.html. Last accessed June 4, 2020.

3. https://www.dea.gov/press-releases/2019/11/04/dea-issues-warning-over-counterfeit-prescription-pills-mexico0. Last accessed June 4, 2020.

4. https://www.medscape.com/viewarticle/460566. Last accessed June 4, 2020.

5. https://www.fda.gov/media/77086/download.

6. https://www.congress.gov/bill/111th-congress/senate-bill/3690. Last accessed June 4, 2020.

7. https://www.c-span.org/video/?295894-4/margaret-hamburg-remarks-counterfeit-perscription-drugs. Last accessed June 4, 2020.

8. https://nabp.pharmacy/newsroom/news/nabp-issues-rogue-online-pharmacy-public-health-alert/. Last accessed June 4, 2020.

9. https://www.accessdata.fda.gov/scripts/cdrh/cfdocs/cfcfr/CFRSearch.cfm?CFRPart=1305&showFR=1&subpartNode=21:9.0.1.1.6.3. Last accessed June 4, 2020.

10. https://scholarlycommons.law.case.edu/cgi/viewcontent.cgi?referer=&httpsredir=1&article=1022&context=jil. Last accessed June 4, 2020.

11. https://en.wikipedia.org/wiki/Sutton%27s_law. Last accessed June 4, 2020.

12. https://www.fda.gov/news-events/press-announcements/statement-fda-commissioner-scott-gottlieb-mdagencys-new-efforts-strengthen-regulation-dietary. Last accessed June 4, 2020.

13. https://www.fda.gov/drugs/counterfeit-medicine/health-care-provider-alert-another-counterfeit-cancermedicine-found-united-states. Last accessed June 4, 2020.

14. https://cmlnetwork.ca/counterfeit-iclusig-ponatinib/. Last accessed June 4, 2020.

15. https://www.theguardian.com/society/2019/feb/12/fake-cancer-drug-made-from-paracetamol-world-healthorganization. Last accessed June 4, 2020.

16. https://www.interpol.int/News-Events/2018/N2018-123. Last accessed June 4, 2020.

17. https://www.healthcarepackaging.com/markets/pharmaceutical/news/13294907/counterfeiters-move-fromlifestyle-drugs-to-lifesaving-drugs. Last accessed June 4, 2020.

18. https://cmpi.org/in-the-news/health-care-chutzpah-vs-health-plan-literacy Last accessed June 4, 2020

19. https://www.taftlaw.com/news-events/law-bulletins/hhs-oig-approves-narrowly-tailored-patient-assistanceprogram. Last accessed June 4, 2020.

20. https://www.cbc.ca/news/thenational/national-today-newsletter-counterfeir-drugs-medicine-1.5014/84. Last accessed June 4, 2020.

21. https://en.wikipedia.org/wiki/Specialty_pharmacy. Last accessed June 4, 2020.

22. https://en.wikipedia.org/wiki/Specialty_drugs_in_the_United_States. Last accessed June 4, 2020.

23. https://www.drugchannels.net/2019/04/the-specialty-pharmacy-boom-our.html. Last accessed June 4, 2020.

24. https://www.dispatch.com/news/20180603/mail-order-pharmacy-system-delays-meds-for-some-patients. Last accessed June 25, 2020.

25. https://www.nola.com/entertainment_life/health_fitness/article_6ad30efb-0cca-5900-90ed62badf5ac35b.html. Last accessed June 25, 2020.

26. https://www.spokesman.com/stories/2018/dec/05/peoples-pharmacy-will-breast-cancer-drug-work-if-s/. Last accessed June 25, 2020.

27. https://www.aniglobalsource.com/blog/serialization-what-it-means-for-pharmaceutical-manufacturing. Last accessed June 4, 2020.

28. https://www.fda.gov/drugs/drug-supply-chain-integrity/drug-supply-chain-security-act-dscsa. Last accessed June 4, 2020.

29. Ibid. Last accessed June 4, 2020.

30. https://www.fda.gov/drugs/drug-supply-chain-security-act-dscsa/title-ii-drug-quality-and-security-act. Last accessed June 4, 2020.

31. https://www.newsweek.com/big-pharma-villain-pbm-569980. Last accessed June 4, 2020.

32. https://www.pewtrusts.org/-/media/assets/2014/04/29/boozallenhamiltonreport.pdf. Last accessed June 4, 2020.

33. https://oig.hhs.gov/oei/reports/oei-05-17-00460.pdf. Last accessed June 4, 2020.

34. https://www.safemedicines.org/2019/01/raid-in-british-columbia-canada-turns-up-a-pill-press-and-over-100-different-pill-dyes.html. Last accessed June 4, 2020.

35. https://www.safemedicines.org/2015/10/5-secrets-canadian-pharmacies-dont-want-you-to-know.html. Last accessed June 4, 2020.

36. https://www.nytimes.com/2004/08/11/us/vermont-will-sue-us-for-the-right-to-import-drugs.html. Last accessed June 4, 2020.

37. http://www.safemedicines.org/wp-content/uploads/FDA-Operation-Reveals-Many-Drugs Promoted-as-_Canadian_-Products-Really-Originate-From-Other-Countries-captured-January-2017.pdf. Last accessed June 4, 2020.

38. https://www.safemedicines.org/2015/11/illinois-and-isaverx.html. Last accessed June 4, 2020.

39. https://www.canada.ca/en/health-canada/corporate/about-health-canada.html. Last accessed June 4, 2020.

40. http://www.safemedicines.org/wp-content/uploads/2018/03/HHS-Report1220.pdf. Last accessed June 4, 2020.

41. https://www.safemedicines.org/2018/07/who-opposes-drug-importation-every-head-of-the-fda-and-hhs-since2000.html. Last accessed June 4, 2020.

42. https://www.hhs.gov/about/news/2019/07/31/hhs-new-action-plan-foundation-safe-importation-certainprescription-drugs.html. Last accessed June 4, 2020.

43. https://www.healthaffairs.org/doi/full/10.1377/hlthaff.20.3.92. Last accessed June 4, 2020.

44. Author's conversations with Canadian government officials.

45. https://www.fda.gov/consumers/consumer-updates/beware-fraudulent-coronavirus-tests-vaccines-andtreatments. Last accessed June 4, 2020.

46. https://www.fda.gov/drugs/drug-supply-chain-integrity/fda-leads-effort-create-supply-chain-security-toolkitmedical-products. Last accessed June 25, 2020.

47. https://www.fda.gov/industry/prescription-drug-user-fee-amendments/pdufa-vi-fiscal-years-2018-2022. Last accessed June 25, 2020.

48. https://www.ncbi.nlm.nih.gov/pmc/articles/PMC6164397/. Last accessed June 4, 2020.

49. https://www.fraserinstitute.org/sites/default/files/pharmaceutical-counterfeiting-endangering-public-healthsociety-and-the-economy.pdf. Last accessed June 4, 2020.

50. https://blogs.scientificamerican.com/molecules-to-medicine/counterfeit-drugs-a-deadly-problem/. Last accessed June 4, 2020.

51. Ibid. Last accessed June 4, 2020.

The Crucial Nature of Intellectual Property

"We cannot negotiate with people who say, 'What's mine is mine and what's yours is negotiable.'" JOHN F. KENNEDY

Some people believe that suspending COVID-19 vaccine patents will expedite the swift development of high quality "cheap" versions of existing vaccines and hasten the pandemic's end. This view is dangerously wrong. Vaccinating the world is essential, but *temporarily* waiving patent rights for COVID-19 vaccines and other innovative therapies (also known as "compulsory licensing") will slow their availability to the developing world.

While providing no gain, compulsory licensing promises lots of pain. Waiving patent protection discourages the cutting-edge research investments that produce breakthrough treatments not just for COVID-19, but for other diseases, like cancer. Weakening these protections would be anti-patient and counterproductive. Patents, specifically, and intellectual property rights more broadly, are a foundational principle upon which healthcare evolution rests.

Waiving COVID-19 Vaccine Patents: A Bad Idea and a Dangerous Precedent

By Peter J. Pitts, Robert Popovian, and Wayne Weingarden

Originally published in the *Journal of Commercial Biotechnology*, September, 2, 2021

Introduction

"Temporarily" waiving biopharmaceutical patent rights (also known as "compulsory licensing")[1] for COVID-19 vaccines is a bad idea — and a dangerous precedent. When it comes to broadening the availability of vaccines, dispensing with patent protection will actually slow their availability to the developing world — and what does "temporary" really mean? Shunting aside patent and intellectual property rights sends a very dangerous signal to innovator biopharmaceutical companies (and their investors) that the government may not be such a good partner after all.

The claim, by India, South Africa, and some high-profile members of civil society (such as Knowledge Ecology International),[2] is that suspending COVID-19 vaccine patents would allow developing countries to manufacture their own "cheap" versions, hastening the end to the pandemic. They're wrong. Dangerously wrong — and entirely unnecessary.

Innovator vaccine developers have been ramping up production for months.[3] It has taken time, industry officials said, because the shots currently available rely on newer technologies like messenger RNA. With the extra output, Pfizer had begun shipping US-produced doses to countries including Mexico and Canada, while Moderna agreed to deliver the COVAXX Initiative doses to supply shots to poor nations.[4]

The companies were also in discussions with the Biden Administration about how to get more supplies to the developing world. The industry proposed providing more doses to developing countries at cost or not for profit, said Jeremy Levin, chairman of the Biotechnology Innovation Organization (BIO) and chief executive of Ovid Therapeutics Inc. "These proposals appear to not even have been looked at."[5]

Gutting IP protections won't make COVID-19 vaccines more readily available but it will set a terrible precedent that will chill future medical innovation and hurt those they are most vociferously claiming to assist. Cui bono?

Biopharmaceutical research is risky and expensive. For every 5,000 molecules developed in the lab, only one successfully advances through lab, animal, and clinical testing and receives regulatory approval.[6] After accounting for all these failures, it costs almost $3 billion, on average, to bring a single medicine to pharmacy shelves.[7]

Biotech investors only take these risks because of strong patent protections.[8] When a startup receives its first patent, the firm's chances of attracting funding from institutional investors — such as venture capitalists — increases 53 percent, according to a National Bureau of Economic Research working paper.[9] Patents save lives and enhance the value of medicines. As Abraham Lincoln (the only president to ever hold a patent) said, "Patents add the fuel of interest to the passion of genius."[10]

Not surprisingly, nations with strong patent laws (and specifically the United States and the European Union) produce higher volumes of new treatments. The United States has the most robust IP protections, which explains why American scientists develop over half of the new drugs invented globally.[11] Waiving patent protection discourages research and development here in America and around the globe.

Patent protections incentivize firms to make big research investments, which in turn produce breakthrough treatments not just for COVID-19, but for other diseases, like cancer. Weakening these protections would be anti-patient and counterproductive. It wouldn't speed the rollout of existing vaccines, but it would ensure we're less prepared to fight the next phase of the COVID-19 pandemic — not to mention future global public health emergencies. This was precisely the strategy behind the Orphan Drug Act of 1983.[12] This major piece of legislation was the first of its kind for rare diseases and its success has helped to encourage similar legislation in other parts of the world. In the late 1970s and early 1980s, there was growing awareness that very few medical treatments were being developed for people who had diseases affecting small patient populations. The problem was that pharmaceutical companies couldn't expect to recover the investment required to develop treatments for diseases affecting a small number of people. Hence, these diseases came to be known as "orphan" diseases.

The Orphan Drug Act provided pharmaceutical manufacturers with three primary incentives: Federal grants for orphan drug research; a 50 percent tax credit to defray the cost of clinical trials; and seven years of marketing exclusivity for products approved as orphans. The result? Currently, more than 400 orphan designated drugs are commercially available and close to 1,000 drugs are undergoing clinical trials.[13] Incentives work, threats do not, and actions have consequences. Incentives drive behavior as do disincentives. One day after President Biden announced his support for a temporary waiver of COVID-19 patent rights, stock prices for innovative biopharmaceutical companies plummeted.

When the power of the healthcare ecosystem (government, biopharmaceutical companies, academia, healthcare providers, logicians, and patients) work together as partners, we accomplish miracles at warp speed. "Waiving" patents isn't good partnership behavior.

Historically, Compulsory Licensing Has Not Worked

Compulsory licensing is legal under international law, but only in limited instances. It allows local companies to produce generic versions of patented medicines in desperate times — such as an infectious disease outbreak. However, India, Brazil, and other nations abuse this policy and allow drugmakers to produce just about any generic without any urgent reason at all, and without the patent owners' permission.[14] "Temporary?" Caveat emptor.

Developing countries obviously need COVID-19 vaccines as quickly as possible. But removing IP protections won't accelerate vaccine distribution in these nations. In fact, it could slow it down. In the past, when developing countries have issued compulsory licenses — which effectively allow domestic manufacturers to create knockoff treatments even before drug patents expire — it has taken years for generic manufacturers to receive the drug formulas, work out logistical and payment challenges, and scale up production. In one case, it took over four years to bring a generic AIDS drug to Rwanda with half that time spent settling a contract between the domestic manufacturer and the patent holder.[15] A valuable lesson learned with direct and immediate application for the COVID-19 patent debate is that patents do not hinder availability, but lack of patent production eviscerates incentives for innovation.

As the late Senator Daniel Patrick Moynihan quipped, "People are entitled to their own opinions, but not to their own facts." Hopefully this reality will result in an open and honest negotiation at the World Trade Organization (WTO) over the next several months, leading up to their Ministerial meeting on November 30. At the May 6, 2021, WTO General Council meeting, Director General Ngozi Okojo Iweala urged members to begin text-based negotiations of the proposed COVID-19 vaccine waiver.[16]

Aren't COVID-19 Vaccines "Essential"?

Vaccinating the world against COVID-19 is essential. But how has the world fared in addressing the accessibility of other "essential medicines"? Considering it's the World Health Organization (WHO) that is driving the policy of pausing COVID-19 vaccine patents, it's worthwhile to examine the impact of that institution's Essential Drug List. The WHO's Model List of Essential Medicines contains the medications considered to be most effective and safe to meet the most important needs in a health system.[17]

Very few of the 400 or so drugs deemed essential are new, or patented (or ever patented) in the world's poorest countries. In category after category, from aspirin to Zithromax, in almost every case and in almost every country, these medicines have always been (or have been for many years) in the public domain. That is, the medicines are fully open to legal and legitimate generic manufacture. Their availability remains spotty and their quality questionable. Just as the coronavirus mutates to survive and thrive, so too do the purveyors of counterfeit medicines. There is no value at all in vaccines that are not manufactured to the highest standards. Poorer nations must receive the same high-quality vaccines that are available in the West. According to a recent report from the Center for Medicine in the Public Interest, "Not surprisingly, the COVID-19 pandemic has increased the public's exposure to counterfeit medical products."[18] Allowing manufacturers with questionable safety records to produce vaccines that require sophisticated processes, procedures, material, and manufacturing is a recipe for disaster.

According to Dr. Michelle McMurry-Heath, the President of BIO, "Handing needy countries a recipe book without the ingredients, safeguards, and sizable workforce needed will not help people waiting for the vaccine. Handing them the blueprint to construct a kitchen that — in optimal conditions — can take a year to build will not help us stop the emergence of dangerous new COVID-19 variants."[19] Dr. Jeremy Levin reinforces the proposition that, "This is not just a matter of forcibly transferring IP and know-how from America to other nations. There was and is no need to rebuild factories around the world where not only will it take a long time to do so but also the standards and capabilities that exist in America cannot be easily replicated or guaranteed. In the future, this decision will act as a disincentive to companies to respond to the next pandemic."[20]

Where Do Medicines Come From?
Many politicians and pundits mistakenly believe that biopharmaceutical innovation is primarily driven by the National Institutes of Health (NIH). The reality is that the primary engine of drug innovation is private industry. The members of the Pharmaceutical Research and Manufacturers Association (PhRMA) spend in excess of $136 billion on research and development — and these are only some of the larger companies.[21]

Both the NIH and private firms provide research financing to academic institutions. But it is industry that employs most of the scientists that conduct the hands-on development work. Unfortunately, some lawmakers have bought the myth that the NIH is primarily responsible for new medicines.

A study by Bhaven N. Sampat and Frank R. Lichtenberg entitled "What Are the Respective Roles of the Public and Private Sectors in Pharmaceutical

Innovation?"[22] provides a data-driven analysis that gives the National Institutes of Health (NIH) its due — but in the proper frame of reference. Sampat and Lichtenberg studied 478 drugs that were associated with $132.7 billion in prescription drug sales in 2006. Less than 10 percent of these drugs had a public-sector patent. Drugs with public-sector patents accounted for just 2.5 percent of sales, although the indirect impact was higher for drugs granted priority review by the FDA. (Priority review is given to drugs that offer major advances in treatment or provide a treatment where no adequate therapy exists.)[23] Drugs whose applications cited federally funded research and development or government publications accounted for 27 percent of sales.

Another study in the *British Medical Journal* also analyzed the topic. Comparable to prior research, the investigators found that the majority of biopharmaceutical research was conducted and funded by the private sector. Despite having excluded vaccines, biologic medicines, and gene therapies from their final analysis, a study limitation noted by the authors, the researchers found that 75 percent of all Food and Drug Administration (FDA) approved drugs between January 2008 and December 2017 were funded and researched by private companies. Only 19 percent of the approved drugs had origins in publicly supported research and development, and 6 percent originated in companies that were spun from publicly supported research programs. Thus, 25 percent of approved medicines benefited from "some" public support. The results were impressive, and indicative of how central private-sector research is to biopharmaceutical innovation.[24]

The Debate Over Remdesivir

Consider remdesivir and the related debate over Bayh/Dole March-in Rights.[25] The recently released Government Accountability Office (GAO) report, "Information on Federal Contributions to Remdesivir,"[26] considered whether federal patent rights were appropriate, given the federal government's contributions in researching and developing the drug.

The GAO report came in response to stiff political headwinds. In August 2020, citing concerns over pricing and availability of remdesivir, 34 state attorneys general (including present Health and US Human Services Secretary Xavier Bercerra) asked federal officials to exercise the government's march-in rights over the COVID19 treatment.[27] The attorneys general said Gilead has been unable to assure a "supply of remdesivir sufficient to alleviate the health and safety needs of the country" amid the COVID-19 pandemic.

The straightforward, unambiguous, and politically inconvenient conclusion of the independent GAO report found that "Federally supported remdesivir research conducted by CDC, DOD, NIH, and NIH-funded universities has not resulted in government patent rights, because, according to agency and university officials, federal contributions to the research did not generate new inventions." The principal investigators at the NIH, who were working on coronavirus research projects, told the GAO they did not consider filing invention disclosures because their work did not involve modifying remdesivir or its parent compound.[28] It was President Franklin Roosevelt who recognized the vital role of the federal government partnering with "Good old American know-how" to win the Second World War and propel the American Century forward. Decades before Operation Warp Speed forged a partnership to defeat a natural foe, an earlier public/private partnership of industry, academia, and government, the Manhattan Project, proved the value of collaboration in the face of a deadly human enemy.

When it comes to regulated healthcare technologies specifically, and the anti-COVID-19 armamentarium explicitly, collaboration is a sine qua non. One of the most important lessons of the pandemic is that when the healthcare ecosystem works together, we can achieve amazing things. We are all in this together. Politics is a distraction. Science must be collegial, intramural, and transnational.

Bad Policy Ideas Have Real-World Consequences

The COVID-19 vaccine debate is not America's first joust with pharmaceutical patents. Senator Bernie Sanders has previously introduced a bill that would replace our current patent system for pharmaceuticals with a "Medical Innovation Prize Fund."[29]

It's not a new idea. The prize model has been used in the past by the old Soviet Union — and it didn't work.[30] The Soviet experience was characterized by low levels of monetary compensation and poor innovative performance. The US experience isn't much better. The federal government paid Robert Goddard (the father of American rocketry) $1,000,000 as compensation for his basic liquid rocket patents.[31] A fair price? Not when you consider that during the remaining life of those patents, US expenditures on liquid-propelled rockets amounted to around $10 billion. This is certainly not what Schumpeter had in mind when he wrote about a "spectacular prize thrown to a small minority of winners." There's a difference between "Creative destruction" and destroying medical innovation.[32]

"Prizes over Patents" legislation would replace a patent system that has allowed the average American life span to increase by almost a full decade over the last 50 years[33] with a prize program that has a solid record of complete failure. To borrow an overused adjective from the world of global climate change — we must protect "sustainable" innovation.

It's important to put the "temporary" COVID-19 vaccine patent waiver in the context of the ongoing battle by the global "anti-pharmaceutical patent" lobby. There is a small but vocal and influential public health policy cohort that believes patents are the most significant cause of healthcare disparities worldwide. Their philosophies repeat and reinforce many misunderstandings relative to the impediments to broader access to medicines. Their ill-considered policy schemes (such as a prize system and a more regular and aggressive use of compulsory licensing practices) reinforce the false narrative of a "Good Guys/Bad Guys" weltanschauung that pits the innovative biopharmaceutical industry against the needs of the developing world. This is untrue, unfortunate, and counterproductive. There are rarely simple answers to complex questions. The reality is that, in order to save the world, we must all work together as partners. A free-market healthcare paradigm for drug development, although far from perfect, works. A well-appointed armamentarium of COVID-19 diagnostic tools, therapeutics, and vaccines — all invented in under one year, speaks to the power of ecosystem teamwork and fair incentives — most importantly patent protection for innovation.

According to a recent article in *Health Affairs*, "The remarkable speed with which we developed diagnostics, therapeutics, and vaccines to combat COVID-19 points to the need for more collaboration, not less. One of the most important lessons of the pandemic is that when the health care ecosystem works together, we can achieve amazing things."[34] And patents are a foundational principle upon which that success rests.

The Biden Administration has empowered a resurgence in the anti-biopharmaceutical industry, anti-patent, anti-intellectual property debate. Shortly after President Biden signaled his support for waiving COVID-19 vaccine patents, Representative Alexandria Ocasio-Cortez tweeted, "Let's do insulin next"[35] and Senator Sanders commented, "This is exactly the kind of leadership the world needs right now ... I also recognize the dedicated work done by activists in communities around the world to put this issue on the global agenda. We are all in this together."[36]

President Biden's support of "temporary" waivers may not end up being so temporary at all if elected officials such as Ocasio-Cortez and Sanders have their way.

Despite this constant negativity from the anti-patent lobby, global production capacity is expanding and accelerating global access is possible. Strengthening the current system that created vaccines and treatments at a record-setting pace is the best way to achieve this important global public health goal. It's time to ask some tough questions: are poorer nations engaged with global manufacturers in negotiating a fair price for vaccines? If not, why not? Have these same developing nations countries thought about partnering with the biopharmaceutical companies to build manufacturing facilities that can legally and safely produce the vaccines — facilities can then be used to manufacture other essential medicines? If we shy away from asking the tough questions, we are unlikely to find the right answers.

While, prima facie, the policy to temporarily waive patent rights seems fair and humanitarian (two words regularly used to describe President Biden), the reality is quite different. Such a policy will not result in a single citizen of the developing world getting vaccinated one minute sooner. The anti-patent consortium is, unfortunately, willing to sacrifice the developing world on its own infallible Altar of Altruism, fueled by their dogmatic adversity to free-market principles.

"The most empowering relationships are those in which each partner lifts the other to a higher possession of their own being." — Pierre Teilhard de Chardin.

REFERENCES

1. https://www.wto.org/english/tratop_e/trips_e/ public_health_faq_e.htm. Last accessed May 8, 2021.

2. https://www.keionline.org/coronavirus. Last accessed May 8, 2021.

3. https://www.wsj.com/articles/covid-19- vaccine-manufacturing-in-u-s-races-ahead11616328001?mod=article. Last accessed May 8, 2021.

4. https://www.wsj.com/articles/moderna-to-delivercovid-19-vaccine-to-hard-hit-developing-world11620037924?mod=article_inline. Last accessed May 8, 2021.

5. https://www.wsj.com/articles/u-ssupport-for-patent-waiver-unlikely-to-costcovid-19-vaccine-makers-in-short-term11620414260?mod=searchresults_pos1&page=1. Last accessed May 8, 2021.

6. https://www.britannica.com/technology/ pharmaceutical-industry/ Drug-discovery-anddevelopment

7. https://pubmed.ncbi.nlm.nih.gov/26928437/. Last accessed May 8, 2021.

8. https://pubs.aeaweb.org/doi/pdf/10.1257/ jep.27.1.23. Last accessed May 8, 2021.

9. https://www.nber.org/papers?page=1&perPage=50 &sortBy=public_date. Last accessed May 8, 2021.

10. https://www.intellectualventures.com/buzz/insights/ president-lincoln-and-the-afire-of-geniusa. Last accessed May 8, 2021.

11. https://www.ncbi.nlm.nih.gov/pmc/articles/PMC2866602/. Last accessed May 8, 2021.

12. https://www.fda.gov/industry/designating-orphan- August 2021 I Volume 26 I Number 2 25 product-drugs-and-biological-products/orphandrug-act-relevant-excerpts. Last accessed May 8, 2021.

13. https://www.fda.gov/patients/rare-diseases-fda. Last accessed May 8, 2021.

14. https://apnews.com/article/dd418a4714854d74a329cfd319946c1c. Last accessed May 8, 2021.

15. https://digitalcommons.law.uga.edu/cgi/ viewcontent.cgi?article=1184&context=jipl. Last accessed May 8, 2021.

16. https://www.wto.org/english/news_e/spno_e/ spno9_e.htm. Last accessed May 8, 2021.

17. https://www.who.int/groups/expert-committee-onselection-and-use-of-essential-medicines/essentialmedicines-lists. Last accessed May 8, 2021.

18. https://www.safemedicines.org/wp-content/ uploads/2019/09/Counterfeits-2020.pdf. Last accessed May 8, 2021.

19. https://go.bio.org/index.php/email/ emailWebview?md_id=28344. Last accessed May 8, 2021.

20. Ibid. Last accessed May 8, 2021.

21. https://www.statista.com/statistics/309466/globalr-and-d-expenditure-for-pharmaceuticals/. Last accessed May 8, 2021.

22. https://www.researchgate.net/ publication/49805993_What_Are_The_ Respective_ Roles_Of_The_Public_And_Private_ Sectors_In_Pharmaceutical_Innovation. Last accessed May 8, 2021.

23. https://www.fda.gov/patients/fast-trackbreakthrough-therapy-accelerated-approval-priorityreview/priority-review. Last accessed May 8, 2021.

24. https://www.bmj.com/content/367/bmj.l5766. Last accessed May 8, 2021.

25. https://fas.org/sgp/crs/misc/R44597.pdf. Last accessed May 8, 2021.

26. https://www.gao.gov/assets/gao-21-272.pdf. Last accessed May 8, 2021.

27. https://www.bizjournals.com/sanfrancisco/ news/2020/08/05/covid-19-coronavirus-gileadremdesivir-march-in.html. Last accessed May 8, 2021.

28. https://www.healthaffairs.org/do/10.1377/ hblog20210421.570435/full/. Last accessed May 8, 2021.

29. https://www.congress.gov/bill/115th-congress/ senate-bill/495/. Last accessed May 8, 2021.

30. https://ojs.stanford.edu/ojs/index.php/intersect/article/view/691. Last accessed May 8, 2021.

31. https://www.nationalmuseum.af.mil/Visit/ Museum-Exhibits/Fact-Sheets/Display/Article/197697/dr-robert-h-goddard/. Last accessed May 8, 2021.

32. https://academyofideas.com/2013/12/the-ethicsof-schopenhauer/. Last accessed May 8, 2021.

33. https://www.health.harvard.edu/blog/whatsin-a-number-looking-at-life-expectancy-in-theus-2020020718871. Last accessed May 8, 2021.

34. https://www.healthaffairs.org/do/10.1377/ hblog20210421.570435/full/. Last accessed May 8, 2021.

35. https://twitter.com/aoc/ status/1390037473472942081. Last accessed May 8, 2021.

36. https://vermontbiz.com/news/2021/may/05/ sanders-supports-biden-backing-covid-19-vaccinewaiver. Last accessed May 8, 2021.

Remdesivir and Federal March-In Rights

By Peter J. Pitts

Originally published in *Health Affairs*, April 30, 2021

The recently released Government Accountability Office (GAO) report, Information on Federal Contributions to Remdesivir, considered whether federal patent rights were appropriate, given the federal government's contributions in researching and developing the drug. The report concluded: Gilead's collaborations with government scientists with respect to remdesivir generated no intellectual property rights for federally funded researchers or government agencies.

This wasn't what those who called for the GAO report wanted or expected to hear. It is relevant to note that one of the loudest voices calling for this study was former California attorney general, now secretary of Health and Human Services, Xavier Becerra.

The GAO report was requested by Congress to provide an independent review of the role the federal government played into researching uses for remdesivir as a treatment for COVID-19. Now known as Veklury, the medicine was the first COVID-19 treatment given an Emergency Use Authorization (EUA) by the Food and Drug Administration (FDA) for treating those at risk for serious manifestations of the virus.

The GAO report came in the face of stiff political headwinds. In August 2020, citing concerns over pricing and availability of remdesivir, 34 state attorneys general asked federal officials to exercise the government's "march-in" rights over the COVID-19 treatment. The attorneys general said Gilead has been unable to assure a "supply of remdesivir sufficient to alleviate the health and safety needs of the country" amid the COVID-19 pandemic. However, for politicians and pundits who regularly paint the innovative biopharmaceutical industry as getting a free ride off the back of government research grants, the GAO report should serve as a wake-up call. When the healthcare ecosystem works together, we can achieve remarkable results at warp speed.

Who "Invents" New Drugs? The Roles of Industry and the NIH

A study by Bhaven N. Sampat and Frank R. Lichtenberg entitled "What Are The Respective Roles Of The Public And Private Sectors In Pharmaceutical Innovation?" provides a data-driven analysis that gives the National Institutes of Health (NIH) its due — but in the proper frame of reference. Sampat and Lichtenberg studied 478 drugs that were associated with $132.7 billion in prescription drug sales in 2006. Less than 10 percent of these drugs had a public-sector patent. Drugs with public-sector patents accounted for just 2.5 percent of sales, although the indirect impact was higher for drugs granted priority review by the FDA. (Priority review is given to drugs that offer major advances in treatment or provide a treatment where no adequate therapy exists.) Drugs whose applications cited federally funded research and development or government publications accounted for 27 percent of sales.

The NIH does play a vital role in basic research and early discovery, but is robbing Productive Peter to pay Government Paul through the ill-considered use of march-in rights the best bang for the buck when it comes to advancing public health? The answer is a clear "no," and the new GAO report on remdesivir reinforces this conclusion.

A Look at the Record

Between 2009 and 2013, Gilead Sciences, Inc. (Gilead) had synthesized the remdesivir compound, conducted and funded preclinical research that first identified and confirmed the antiviral activity of remdesivir and its parent compound against coronaviruses and other viruses, and had begun patenting the compounds.

Between 2013 and 2020, the Centers for Disease Control and Prevention (CDC), the Department of Defense (DOD), and the NIH conducted and funded preclinical research collaborations that helped to demonstrate remdesivir's antiviral properties against multiple viruses, and the three NIH-funded clinical trials supplemented but did not replace Gilead's ongoing research activities. (See exhibit 1 for examples of federal support.)

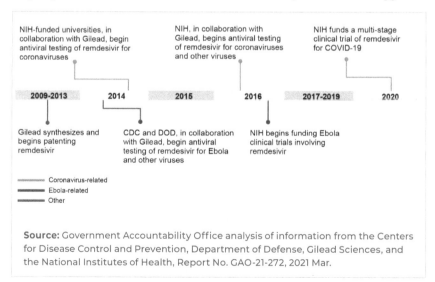

Source: Government Accountability Office analysis of information from the Centers for Disease Control and Prevention, Department of Defense, Gilead Sciences, and the National Institutes of Health, Report No. GAO-21-272, 2021 Mar.

As of December 2020, federal funding for preclinical studies and clinical trials involving remdesivir totaled about $162 million, as follows: $109.2 million for NIH-funded clinical trials; $39.7 million for DOD's preclinical research; $11.9 million for preclinical research conducted by the NIH and NIH-funded universities; and; $0.7 million for the CDC's preclinical research.

The straightforward, unambiguous, and politically inconvenient conclusion of the independent GAO report found that "Federally supported remdesivir research conducted by CDC, DOD, NIH, and NIH-funded universities has not resulted in government patent rights, because, according to agency and university officials, federal contributions to the research did not generate new inventions." The principal investigators at the NIH, who were working on coronavirus research projects, told the GAO they did not consider filing invention disclosures because their work did not involve modifying remdesivir or its parent compound.

In addition, Gilead entered research collaborations with federal agencies and universities with a portfolio of existing patents and patent applications, including for the remdesivir compound, which would have left little room for the federal agencies to generate their own patents. For example, the GAO report cites that DOD officials told them that when DOD scientists performed antiviral testing of remdesivir against Ebola virus, they used standard tests and screening methods and did not come up with either new tests or methods.

The GAO noted that NIH scientists did not submit invention disclosures from their remdesivir research, and invention disclosures were unlikely to be filed, because Gilead had already determined remdesivir was useful in treating coronaviruses before the NIH began its research. NIH officials told the GAO that, given these circumstances, the NIH did not conduct an inventorship analysis.

The majority of federally funded research supported a clinical trial of remdesivir for the treatment of COVID-19 after the emergence of SARS-CoV-2 (nearly a decade after Gilead invented remdesivir), which proceeded in parallel with Gilead's sponsored COVID-19 clinical trials.

The Urgency of Collaborative Science

The GAO report is clear, and it will make many people unhappy. But this doesn't mean that public-private partnerships serve no use. On the contrary, they are more important now than ever before.

It was President Franklin Roosevelt who recognized the vital role of the federal government partnering with "Good old American know-how" to win the Second World War and propel the American Century forward.

Decades before Operation Warp Speed forged a partnership to defeat a natural foe, an earlier public-private partnership of industry, academia, and government, the Manhattan Project, proved the value of collaboration in the face of a deadly human enemy.

On November 17, 1944, President Roosevelt wrote to Vannevar Bush, the director of the three-year-old Office of Scientific Research and Development, "New frontiers of the mind are before us, and if they are pioneered with the same vision, boldness, and drive with which we have waged this war we can create a fuller and more fruitful employment and a fuller and more fruitful life." As Bush responded to the president in his 1945 report, "Science: The Endless Frontier": "Science can be effective in the national welfare only as a member of a team, whether the conditions be peace or war. But without scientific progress no amount of achievement in other directions can insure our health, prosperity, and security as a nation in the modern world."

When it comes to regulated healthcare technologies specifically, and the anti-COVID-19 armamentarium explicitly, collaboration is a sine qua non. Politics is a distraction. Science must be collegial, intramural, and transnational.

The remarkable speed with which we developed diagnostics, therapeutics, and vaccines to combat COVID-19 points to the need for more collaboration, not less. Just because those who called for the federal government to exercise march-in rights for remdesivir didn't get their way doesn't mean they should pick up their marbles and go home. One of the most important lessons of the pandemic is that when the healthcare ecosystem works together, we can achieve amazing things. We are all in this together. The two-dimensional "Good Guys/Bad Guys" approach is simplistic and deleterious to advancing the public health. There are rarely simple answers to complex questions. As H.L. Mencken reminds us, "For every complex problem there is an answer that is clear, simple, and wrong." Remdesivir march-in rights fall into this category.

The Devil Is in the Details
The government report demonstrates that Gilead's significant investment in the drug, which exceeded $1 billion in 2020 alone, far outweighs the federal funding associated with remdesivir-related research identified by the GAO.

Footnote 35 on page 15 details Gilead's investment of more than $930 million in remdesivir-related research and development, including $786 million in Gilead-funded research and development and $147 million to supply remdesivir at no cost for use in clinical and research settings. For those who demand that march-in rights "follow the money," it's important to recognize what that means and where it leads. As Oscar Wilde quipped, "the truth is seldom pure and never simple." If "science is back," let's all of us follow the science.

CHAPTER FIVE

Science Is Back

"Science perfects genius and moderates that fury of the fancy that cannot contain itself within the bounds of reason."

JOHN DRYDEN

"We must follow the science" has been the global battle cry in the war against COVID-19. Bravo. But "following the science" means that we must accept where it leads us — and that isn't always socially, politically, or ethically palatable — or expedient. If "science is back," it means we must embrace the fact that healthcare innovation is difficult and expensive and cannot be rushed to suit outside agendas. (A triple play of political and corporate inconvenience.) Importantly, we must avoid the salve of simple answers to complex questions (*hydroxychloroquine! ivermectin!* etc.). Science is filled with uncertainties. Welcome to science, our expert guide whether we're dealing with mRNA vaccines, CRISPR technology, genetic testing, or advances in treatments for both acute and chronic diseases.

Understanding CRISPR

By Gregory Katz and Peter J. Pitts

Originally published in the *Morning Consultant*, September 18, 2017

Cancer survivors strive to rebuild their lives despite the many obstacles they face in obtaining bank loans, resuming their careers, or finding reasonably priced insurance policies. Many wish to have children but are concerned about passing on their genetic predispositions to their offspring. Why not directly edit cancer survivors' DNA in order to rid them of these mutations and eradicate the possibility of passing it on to the next generation? With recent developments in genome editing — including technologies such as clustered regularly interspaced short palindromic repeats — genetically modifying cancer predispositions is closer to practical science than science fiction.

Cancer survivors can carry mutations that will be transmitted to their children. Today, many of these mutations have been identified and can be tracked. With the recent development of genome editing technologies and CRISPR the possibility of genetically modifying the human germline (gametes and embryos) has never been closer. This perspective has sparked a controversy within the scientific community with reactions ranging from calls for a ban on modification, to cautious approval of further research.

The debate over CRISPR-based engineering is generally framed from an ethical and scientific perspective. The economic dimension is often overlooked. CRISPR will both create and meet demands on the individual and collective levels. Economic stakeholders — biotech and medtech firms, public payers, health insurers, fertility clinics, parents-to-be, cancer survivors, their relatives and offspring — may share converging interests in preventing the spread of cancer predispositions in the human population.

The use of CRISPR on nonviable human embryos has sparked a sense of urgency in the scientific community. In reaction, an international summit was hosted in December 2015 by the US National Academy of Sciences, the Chinese Academy of Sciences, and the Royal Society of the UK, in order to issue a warning statement on human germ cell manipulation. The statement calls for a cautiousness on genome editing of human germlines for reproductive purposes. It invokes several arguments such as the risk of technical error; responsibility toward the future generations that will inherit these modifications; the difficulty in reversing the modifications once they have been introduced and disseminated in the population; the possibility that genetic improvements will only concern a subset of the population, thereby exacerbating social inequities; the ethical and moral considerations in purposely altering human evolution.

The technical risk argument is legitimate — but as with all biotechnological breakthroughs, the risk could decrease through scientific advances.

The risk of exacerbating social inequities is an argument commonly put forward regarding the introduction of new technologies that are costly. Yet the low cost of CRISPR could allow healthcare systems to propose it under universal coverage, thereby ensuring equal access to all in the name of social justice.

Another argument invokes the moral responsibility of purposely altering human evolution. But what do we mean by "human evolution"? This argument appears to assume, on the one hand, that human evolution is simply the evolution of the genome, and on the other hand, that the human genome in its natural state cannot be perfected. If we extrapolate this logic, shouldn't doctors feel guilty about their everyday attempts to cure natural disorders affecting the human body? Shouldn't the centuries-long endeavor to extend life expectancy be considered a clear interference in the natural evolution of humanity?

CRISPR illustrates what the economist Joseph Schumpeter coined "creative destruction": Genome-editing technologies could carry "everlasting storms of innovations" that will disrupt market structures. Eventually, CRISPR could drastically alleviate the economic burden of cancer by revolutionizing two models currently used by healthcare systems: cancer screening programs, and precision medicine.

The prevention strategy used by health policymakers to fight cancer mainly consists of cancer screening programs to detect tumors as early as possible and rapidly begin treatment. But with CRISPR, prevention campaigns would make it possible to intervene even earlier, detecting and correcting genetic mutations before they produce tumors. CRISPR could make it possible to eradicate close to 3,600 rare monogenic disorders caused by identified genes.

CRISPR could turn this century into a huge wave of genome decontamination. Like the carbon footprint, a genomic footprint disseminated in the general population could be taxed as a prejudice to the common good. CRISPR would make it possible to decontaminate a population's reproductive cells. One could choose not to do so — in the name of individual freedom — but this would spawn a new kind of polluter payer tax, since parents would be taking the risk of disseminating harmful genes in the general population, potentially resulting in costly treatments for the community at large.

Public opinion surveys show that most Americans are in favor of genome editing to prevent their children from inheriting serious disease, though 65 percent consider that modifying the genes of unborn children should not be legalized. Another survey conducted in 2016 found that 49 percent of Americans approve of the use of germline editing to reduce the transmission of hereditary diseases. A caveat to these surveys is that they were conducted in the general population, where cancer survivors statistically represent only a small fraction. In these days of "patient-centricity," it would have been interesting to compare the survey results of the general population with a sample of cancer patients and their families.

CRISPR could lead to the emergence of what Nietzsche called "the grand politics [which] places physiology above all other questions — it wants to rear humanity as a whole, it measures the range of the races, of peoples, of individuals according to the guarantee of life that they carry within them." In the CRISPR century, this vision is probably not a prophecy but a possible future.

Implications of CRISPR-Based Germline Engineering for Cancer Survivors

By Gregory Katz and Peter J. Pitts

Originally published in *Therapeutic Innovation & Regulatory Science,* August 18, 2017

Introduction

Cancer survivors strive to rebuild their lives despite the many obstacles they face in obtaining bank loans, resuming their careers, or finding reasonably priced insurance policies.[1] Many wish to have children but are concerned about passing on their genetic predispositions to cancer to their offspring. Why not directly edit the cancer survivors' germline DNA to rid them of these mutations and preserve their lineage?

Our understanding of the biology of cancer has expanded exponentially in the last decade, and with it the awareness of its extreme complexity. With cancer's basis in genomics now established, there have been extensive efforts to characterize the main driver mutations and biological pathways, especially through The Cancer Genome Atlas (TCGA).[2,3] In a review of the cancer genome landscape, 84 known oncogenes and 54 tumor suppressor genes have been fully validated.[4] Unquestionably there will be more; the total number of genes involved in pivotal mutations is estimated at close to 200.[5] However, with the recent development of genome-editing technologies such as CRISPR, genetically modifying cancer predispositions has never been closer.

Genome-editing techniques allow the custom-synthesis of DNA fragments — the insertion, deletion, or expression of genetic variants in a targeted, simple, and efficient manner.[6] The most recent version of these molecular cut-and-paste technologies, CRISPR is based on two components — an enzyme (Cas9) that functions like molecular scissors, cutting out certain genes while inserting others, and an RNA molecule that guides these scissors toward a specific DNA sequence.[7] Other techniques exist, such as Zinc Finger Nucleases (ZFN) and Transcription Activator-Like Effector Nucleases (TALENs), but today CRISPR engineering stands out through its speed, accuracy, ease of use, and low cost.[8]

Genome editing already has a wide range of applications in infectiology, the prevention of new HIV infections,[9] and the neutralization of malaria-carrying mosquitoes;[10] in agriculture, with the transgenic editing of rice,[11] oranges,[12] transgenic livestock[13] and hypoallergenic chickens;[14] in pharmacology, with the production of organoids that can accelerate cancer drug screening;[15] and in biomedicine, to correct mutations that can cause hereditary diseases[16] such as Duchenne muscular dystrophy,[17–19] cataracts,[20] hereditary deafness,[21] beta thalassemia,[22] and cystic fibrosis.[23,24]

In oncology, genome-editing technologies are already being applied in a wave of clinical trials to conditions ranging from leukemia.[25] metastatic non–small cell lung cancer[26] and melanoma, to sarcoma and myeloma.[27] All these clinical trials are conducted on somatic cells, but CRISPR is already being considered for use on germline stem cells, which could make it possible to modify the DNA of spermatogonial stem cells.[28] Genome engineering of spermatogonial stem cells would free descendants from the symptoms of the targeted disease.[29,30] It would also ensure that individuals would not become asymptomatic carriers of these mutations that, from an epidemiological standpoint, would significantly decrease the disease's frequency in the human population.[31] In theory, these mutations could eventually disappear over generations, thereby eradicating hereditary diseases whose main genetic markers have been identified, such as cystic fibrosis and Huntington's disease.

The debate over CRISPR-based germline engineering is generally framed from an ethical and scientific perspective. The economic dimension is often overlooked. In this editorial, we analyze the industrialization of this technology and anticipate that CRISPR will both create and meet demands on the individual and collective levels. Economic stakeholders — biotech and medtech firms, public payers, health insurers, fertility clinics, parents-to-be, cancer survivors, their relatives and offspring — may share converging interests in preventing the spread of cancer predispositions in the human population.

From Hereditary Risk Assessment to Clinical Interventions

Cancer is a genetic disease whose pathogenesis is influenced by hereditary and environmental factors. Genetic susceptibility and predisposition to cancer depend on the penetrance of the inherited germline and allele mutations, which are classified in three groups: high, moderate/intermediate, and low. Low penetrance alleles predispose carriers to cancer risks that are slightly higher than those observed in the general population. Moderate penetrance alleles increase the risk of disease by a factor of roughly two to five.[32] High penetrance alleles predispose an individual to the risk of cancer throughout their life, with a risk often 10 times that observed in the general population. This is the case of colorectal cancer, for which 5 percent of cases can be explained by germline mutations in high penetrance alleles such as APC, MLH1, or MSH2.[33] For breast cancer, BRCA1 and BRCA2 susceptibility genes are involved in roughly 25 percent of cases of families affected by hereditary breast cancer. For carriers of these genes, the assessed cumulative risk of breast cancer at age 80 is approximately 80 percent.[34]

The following question therefore arises: what would the clinically acceptable risk threshold be for using CRISPR to prevent the transmission of alleles associated with cancer? Should usage be strictly limited to high or intermediate penetrance alleles? While low penetrance alleles correspond to a polygenic model in which many of them are tied to a very low genotypic risk (factor of 1.5 to 2), their accumulation can have a multiplier effect on susceptibility in the general population.[35] Thus, individuals carrying a large number of low penetrance alleles may be exposed to a cumulative risk of cancer of close to 50 percent throughout their lifetime — hence the importance of identifying low penetrance alleles that are responsible for genetic susceptibility.[36] In other words, even for low penetrance alleles, genome editing could theoretically have a clinical utility both for cancer patients and their descendants who may inherit these predispositions.[32]

One possible usage of CRISPR to prevent hereditary cancers would involve a multidisciplinary approach to assess the probabilities of germline mutations in cancer-susceptibility genes, and then cross-checking these probabilities with the history of an individual and their family. The possible identification of Variants of Uncertain Significance (VUS) further complicates the outlook for genome editing, and although next-generation sequencing technologies will probably help to gradually reduce the number of VUSs, for the time being the use of CRISPR reflects an ethics of uncertainty.[37]

Although the utilization of CRISPR is still experimental for cancer patients, several investigational protocols may prefigure targeted therapeutic approaches in oncology. In a clinical trial for metastatic non–small cell lung cancer, a Chinese team from Sichuan University is extracting immune T cells from the patient's blood and using CRISPR technology to knock out a specific gene that encodes a protein called PD-1, which normally blocks the cell's capacity to launch an immune response.[26] The edited cells will then be multiplied in vitro and reintroduced into the patient's bloodstream, where they are expected to target cancer cells. Although CRISPR-Cas9 can result in edits at the wrong places in the genome — with potentially harmful effects — the US National Institutes of Health's (NIH's) Recombinant DNA Advisory Committee issued a positive recommendation in 2016 for a similar study designed to combine gene editing and immunotherapy to treat melanoma, myeloma, and sarcoma.[27]

In practice, before using CRISPR germline editing on carriers of cancer predispositions, the technology's analytical and clinical validity needs to be demonstrated, as does its clinical utility, that is, its capacity to accurately and reproducibly target one type of cancer over several generations. Such a demonstration represents a tremendous challenge, especially since the clinical utility of genetic testing for moderate penetrance genes is still a controversial issue.[38] This demonstration must meet the requirements of the Evaluation of Genomic Applications in Practice and Prevention (EGAPP) drawn up by the US Centers for Disease Control and Prevention and used by many health care systems, as well as the American Society of Clinical Oncology (ASCO).[39] EGAPP establishes four evaluation criteria that could apply to CRISPR: analytic validity, clinical validity, clinical utility, and ethical, legal, and social issues. To some extent, the clinical utility of CRISPR-based germline engineering could be compared with artificial reproductive technologies currently used to prevent the transmission of cancer predispositions in families at risk. Validating CRISPR's clinical utility would require demonstrating that this approach leads to improved clinical outcomes and enhanced quality of life, which represent added value not only for patients but also for asymptomatic carriers of cancer predispositions and their descendants.

Rectifying or Altering Our Inheritable Genome

While the ethical debate has revealed a relative consensus on the use of CRISPR on somatic cells for scientific or therapeutic purposes, no such common ground has been reached on the issue of modifying human germlines.[40,41] Countries such as Japan, China, and India forbid it through declarations that are legally nonbinding,[42,43] while the Council of Europe has made its prohibition a legal requirement for its member states.[44] In 2015, the United Kingdom (UK) drew attention by authorizing the manipulation of gametes carrying mitochondrial DNA defects, which is a type of intervention on the human germline.[45]

The use of CRISPR on nonviable human embryos has sparked a sense of urgency in the scientific community.[46] In reaction, an international summit was hosted in December 2015 by the US National Academy of Sciences, the Chinese Academy of Sciences, and the Royal Society of the UK to issue a warning statement on human germ cell manipulation.[47] The statement calls for a cautiousness on genome editing of human germlines for reproductive purposes. It invokes several arguments such as the risk of technical error; responsibility toward the future generations that will inherit these modifications; the difficulty in reversing the modifications once they have been introduced and disseminated in the population; the possibility that genetic improvements will only concern a subset of the population, thereby exacerbating social inequities; and the ethical and moral considerations in purposely altering human evolution.

Following the reading of the statement, a participant in the audience — a mother of a child suffering from a genetic disorder — spoke out, describing the disease and how it destroyed the life of her son and her family, concluding with "if you have the skills and the knowledge to fix these diseases, then do it."[48] Moratoriums and prohibitions have a hard time standing up to the real-life experiences of patients and their families when they challenge the arguments against germline modification.

The *technical risk* argument is legitimate, but as with all biotechnological breakthroughs, the risk could decrease through scientific advances. Over time, technological improvements in CRISPR could reduce the occurrence of off-target edits, and certain genetic interactions with the environment.

The argument of responsibility toward future generations is not as obvious as it may initially seem — future generations could just as well be indignant that nothing was attempted to prevent the transmission of genetic mutations that could potentially have been eliminated with CRISPR. Some invoke the argument that these germline modifications would be made without the consent of future generations.[49] But isn't this already the case for other commonly used techniques such as In Vitro Fertilization (IVF) and Intra-Cytoplasmic Sperm Injection (ICSI)? No parent has ever obtained the prior consent of their unborn children when deciding to bring them to life, and no children have ever consented to accepting the genetic endowment of their progenitors.

Inspired by the precautionary principle, which states that nothing must be done unless everything is completely understood, the argument that genome alterations are irreversible is based on the assumption that their widespread dissemination cannot be undone. But why couldn't genome editing work in both directions, like a dynamic word processor with corrective mechanisms? Technically, with CRISPR, previously removed or modified mutations can be reintroduced into the genome.[50] Reversing the modifications introduced by CRISPR would theoretically enable backtracking and correcting any biosafety accidents, which would meet the provisions of the precautionary principle.[51]

The risk of exacerbating social inequities is an argument commonly put forward regarding the introduction of new technologies that are costly. Yet the low cost of CRISPR could allow healthcare systems to propose it under universal coverage, thereby ensuring equal access to all in the name of social justice.[52]

The final argument invokes the moral responsibility of purposely altering human evolution. But what do we mean by "human evolution"? This argument appears to assume, on the one hand, that human evolution is simply the evolution of the genome, and on the other hand, that the human genome in its natural state cannot be perfected. If we extrapolate this logic, shouldn't doctors feel guilty about their everyday attempts to cure natural disorders affecting the human body? Shouldn't the centuries-long endeavor to extend life expectancy be considered a clear interference in the natural evolution of humanity?

The prenatal diagnosis of breast cancer illustrates the potential impact of CRISPR on healthcare systems. Since 2009, the British health authorities have been genetically screening embryos created through in vitro fertilization (IVF) for families with a history of breast cancer.[53] As in many countries, in the UK the National Health Services covers the cost of this procedure, which is invasive and risky for women because it involves ovarian stimulation to collect the oocytes,[54] and for unborn children because the IVF technique combined with intracytoplasmic sperm injection (ICSI) can cause premature births with an increased prevalence of congenital disorders.[55] The recent introduction of the noninvasive prenatal diagnosis (NIPD) allows the DNA circulating in a mother's blood to be analyzed to detect aneuploidy in a fetus while limiting iatrogenic risks for both mother and child.[56] In general, health professionals view NIPD as a positive advance in prenatal diagnosis.[57] However, although some urge caution in the use of NIPD to detect BRCA1 and BRCA2 genes in unborn children, other health professionals believe that NIPD offers parents-to-be who already have a disease the guarantee that it will not be passed on to their descendants.[58]

As a disruptive approach, genome editing could eventually eclipse standard birth screening techniques if CRISPR succeeds in eliminating BRCA mutations from the parents' germline. It would also avoid creating surplus embryos and destroying the affected ones. Genome-editing technologies usher in a preventive logic that is similar in some respects to vaccination campaigns that seek to gradually eradicate a targeted disease in a population. The use of CRISPR could gradually prevent the dissemination of BRCA genes in the population, avoiding hundreds of thousands of hereditary cancers, and ruined lives, while relieving healthcare systems from a significant proportion of the heavy economic burden of cancer.

The Economic Burden of Cancer

Numerous studies have assessed the considerable socioeconomic impact of cancer, in particular the financial burden for patients[59,60] as the result of their loss of employment or productivity at work.[61,62] The financial repercussions of cancer also impact access to care and the survivor's capacity to meet the basic necessities of everyday life.[63] A further factor is the frequent inability of insolvent patients to pay for the cost of cancer-related medical expenses not covered by their insurance.[64] The difficulty in obtaining insurance coverage exacerbates the financial distress of survivors, in some cases leading to a deterioration in health or even a higher mortality rate.[65,66]

Beyond the individual challenges encountered by survivors, cancer represents a tremendous economic burden on healthcare systems. In the United States, the NIH evaluated the cost of treating cancer in 2010 at $125 billion, and project the 2020 cost at $207 billion.[67] In 2012, the total cost of cancer in the 28 countries of the European Union was €143 billion, of which 40 percent was directly tied to care.[68,69]

Healthcare systems are struggling to keep up with these soaring costs, especially for anticancer drugs. "High cancer drug prices are affecting the care of patients with cancer and our healthcare system," declared a patient-driven initiative and petition to curb prices of anticancer drugs.[70] In 2015, the average gross household income in the US was $56,000 per year.[71] For an insured patient with cancer who needs a drug that costs $120,000 per year, "the out-of-pocket expenses could be as much as $30,000 — more than half their average household income," according to the authors of the petition. The average price of new cancer drugs has risen between 5- and 10-fold over 15 years to more than $100,000 a year in 2012. As a result of these rising prices, the cost of drugs for each additional year lived rose from $54,000 in 1995 to $207,000 in 2013.[72]

How is this price escalation justified? Fortunately, technological disruptions often result in lower prices. In genomics, next generation sequencing (NGS) technologies have enabled an exponential drop in sequencing costs, which fell from $100 million in 2001 to approximately $1000 in 2016.[73] This same phenomenon could occur with CRISPR: at €34.4 per genetic target, CRISPR costs 10 times less than RNAi technology (€337.0 per target) and 64 times less than TALEN technology (€2.360 per target).[74] In terms of technological performance, CRISPR-Cas9 has already leapfrogged TALEN technology, mostly because Cas9 offers an unprecedented simplicity to target a large variety of functional domains to various genomic sites.[75] While RNAi has dominated the mammalian gene expression manipulation field for the past 15 years, the recent rapid growth of CRISPR-Cas9 raises the question of whether RNAi will become a tool of the past.[76]

CRISPR illustrates what the economist Joseph Schumpeter coined "creative destruction": genome-editing technologies could carry "everlasting storms of innovations" that will disrupt market structures.[77] Eventually, CRISPR could drastically alleviate the economic burden of cancer by revolutionizing two models currently used by healthcare systems: cancer screening programs and precision medicine.

The prevention strategy used by health policymakers to fight cancer mainly consists in cancer screening programs to detect tumors as early as possible and rapidly begin treatment. But with CRISPR, prevention campaigns would make it possible to intervene even earlier, detecting and correcting genetic mutations before they produce tumors. This would offset the costs of periodic screening exams (e.g., mammographies, colonoscopies) and the treatments (e.g., chemotherapies, radiotherapies). With germline engineering, CRISPR could also offset the costs of artificial reproductive technologies for cancer survivors who wish to give birth to cancer-free children (e.g., IVF, ICSI, preimplantation genetic diagnosis).

For colorectal cancer, population-based screening programs are evaluated in terms of budget impact and cost effectiveness.[78] In Australia, for instance, a study shows that — at AU$12,405 per life-year gained and an average life-time expectancy of 16.084 years — five-yearly colonoscopy screening was the most cost-effective strategy.[79] Medico-economic evaluations have also been conducted in other countries such as Belgium, with similar results.[80] Currently based on the early detection and treatment of colorectal cancer, these public health strategies could be upended by CRISPR. Rather than investing in a national colonoscopy program, budgets could be reallocated to edit genomes in the population — in particular for families at risk — with a view to eliminating the main hereditary predispositions of colorectal cancer in order to reduce its prevalence and eradicate its transmission to future generations.

CRISPR could also profoundly transform the present model of precision medicine and eventually achieve the aim of making medicine an art of precision. According to the 2008 definition of the US Office of Science and Technology, "precision medicine classifies patients into subpopulations that differ in their susceptibility to a particular disease, in the biology and/ or prognosis of those diseases that may develop, or in their response to a specific treatment."[81] Is this approach cost-effective? Oncotype Dx is an example of a molecular assay with a putative value-based price of $3,500 per test.[82] The major economic benefit is that it avoids chemotherapy costs and side effects (including the risk of death) in women with early stage breast cancer by identifying women with a very low risk of cancer recurrence.[83] In England, Oncotype Dx was recommended for use by NICE based on a calculation that took account of the QALY health gains from avoiding the adverse effects of chemotherapy, as well as the savings from reduced treatment cost.[84] In France, Oncotype Dx was also found cost-effective from a national insurance perspective (€2134 per QALY gained) and cost saving from a societal perspective (€602 lower than costs of standard care).[85] The approach based on value assessment in precision cancer medicine could simply disappear if CRISPR is able to eliminate the main genetic predispositions to breast cancer. If so, the disease will no longer be triggered, rendering companion diagnostics and costly treatments pointless.

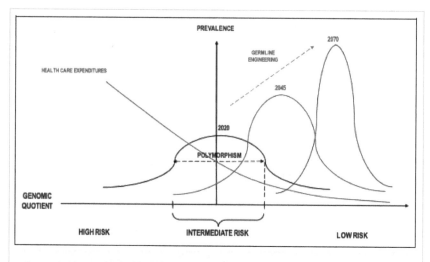

Figure 1: The genomic quotient (GQ). The GQ would be calculated by comparing the average number of pathogenic variants in a population with that of an individual. The GQ score would integrate parameters such as variant profiles and levels of penetrance. Over generations, use of germline genome editing would gradually skew the bell curve to the right, increasing the average quotient of the population and lowering health care costs, but also narrowing the population's polymorphism and impoverishing genetic diversity between humans.

The Genomic Quotient

CRISPR could make it possible to eradicate close to 3,600 rare monogenic disorders caused by identified genes.[86] Theoretically, this perspective could also be extended to polygenic disorders such as cancer, with a higher level of complexity and unpredictability in terms of clinical outcomes. For each individual, assessing genetic risks will progressively mean establishing a series of scorecards at different periods in time, based on genetic predispositions, lifestyle, and exposure to epigenetic factors. As new genetic markers and their penetrance are gradually identified, it may eventually become possible to evaluate the genomic quotient of an individual, that is, the morbidity risks of a given genome based on the mutations it contains.[87] The genomic quotient — a composite score similar to the intellectual quotient — could contribute to stratify risk-adjusted profiles statistically distributed in the homogeneous subpopulations.[88] The genomic quotient of each profile would be given an economic value based partly on the risk of a disease appearing and partly on the cost of the treatments required to cure the disease (see Figure 1). As with the actuarial models used in the insurance industry, it would become possible to observe that people with a high genomic quotient get sick less often than the average person, implying lower healthcare costs, and vice versa.

The genomic quotient would help target individuals for whom CRISPR-based germline engineering would provide medical and economic added value. Such an approach could bring about a significant decrease in healthcare costs within two to three generations. The phenomenon could be accelerated through positive and negative eugenics programs where high quotients would receive economic incentives to procreate — such as tax credits or low health insurance premiums — and low quotients would be economically penalized if they refused to eliminate the cancer predispositions of their germline DNA.

This scenario would have profound consequences, as this normative approach toward human births would reduce the polymorphism of a population in a few generations, potentially putting the survival of the human species at risk. For instance, certain genetic disorders confer resistance to infectious diseases: sickle-cell anemia provides resistance to malaria, cystic fibrosis to cholera, Niemann-Pick disease type C1 prevents the filovirus infection, and Tay-Sachs disease provides protection against tuberculosis.[89] Using CRISPR to eradicate genetic disease variants would imply greater exposure of human species to infectious diseases. This genomic stratification associated with a risk classification is reminiscent of the concept of "the average man" introduced in 1844 by Adolphe Que'telet in his work on anthropometry and body mass index.[90] Today, health insurance is moving toward establishing the concept of "average genome," associated with nosological risks arranged in low-, intermediate-, and high-risk homogeneous groups.[91] From the insurance perspective, the average genome would represent the average risk that actuarial models would consider reasonable to cover, in the name of solidarity.[92]

Eugenic Freedom for All

With CRISPR technologies comes the resurgence of eugenics, with the instrumental capability to select humans based on their phenotypic and/ or genotypic profiles. But who would dare to proclaim which hereditary standards are acceptable within a population? The State? "The individual," answers Nobel Laureate James Watson: "Eugenics is [a way to] self-correct your evolution, and the message I have is that individuals should direct the evolution of their descendants: don't let the State do it. I think it would be irresponsible not to direct your evolution if you could, in the sense that you could have a healthy child versus an unhealthy child."

In Antiquity, Plato's Republic recommended aristocratic eugenics designed to favor mating between men and women of the elite. In the 20th century, the Third Reich combined positive eugenics (lebensborn) with negative eugenics (the final solution) to promote the Aryan phenotype. With CRISPR, a new kind of eugenics could emerge in modern democracies, this time based not on social or phenotypic criteria but rather on a genotypic evaluation combining morbidity rate and economic burden. Genomic standard profiles would be defined by the citizens themselves. The State's power would be limited to guaranteeing eugenic freedom for all, without interfering in the private reproductive choices of its citizens.

Today, Great Britain illustrates this kind of approach by regularly updating an official list of hereditary diseases for which newborn genetic screening is authorized and reimbursed. In 2004, the Human Fertilization and Embryology Authority (HFEA) had included 29 diseases, including Huntington's disease and Tay-Sachs disease. By January 2017, there were 415 diseases on the list, including breast, colon, and ovarian cancer, as well as other illnesses, many of which are treatable, poorly penetrant, and late-onset diseases. Within 13 years, the number of diseases for which newborn genetic screening is reimbursed increased by a factor of 14.

"Have your say on conditions awaiting consideration," the HFEA website announces: through a citizen's forum, patients and their families can make their voice heard and weigh in on the inclusion of new genetic diseases in the list, such as albinism type 2. In a sense, this list sets a limit, yet at the same time, by allowing citizens to participate in the consultation, this limit is elastic and slippery. With this democratic approach, the State is not imposing eugenic norms on its citizens; it is giving them the freedom to choose the genomes they consider undesirable for the next generation.

But with CRISPR-based germline technologies, what will happen if some people refuse to decontaminate their descendants' genomes? Could the State decide to no longer pay for their children's treatment if they suffer from a hereditary disease? The estimated cost for the treatment of stage IV melanoma is up to $152,244 per year and per patient: how many families could afford such an expense? In this scenario, parents would have the choice to use or refuse CRISPR in theory, but in practice, the economic consequences of their refusal would be prohibitive.

Industrializing Germinal Decontamination
CRISPR is at the crossroads of the healthcare and agri-food industries. Startup companies such as Caribou Biosciences, CRISPR Therapeutics, Intellia Therapeutics, and Editas Medicine have provided private equity financing for Cas9-based genome engineering firms. In all, companies with an interest in using Cas9 for applications related to gene therapy have raised more than $600 million in venture capital and public markets between 2013 and 2015.[93] The pace of this activity is remarkable given that the first granted patent for the use of CRISPR in eukaryotic cells was issued on April 14, 2014. In 2015, several high-profile investors, including the Bill & Melinda Gates Foundation and Google Ventures, invested $120 million in the genome-editing firm Editas Medicine.[94]

In October 2016, there were 1625 CRISPR-related inventions distributed in five main technical categories: components (CRISPR RNA, Cas9 enzyme, etc.), activity (Cas cleavage, etc.), vectors (bacterial, viral, plasmid), delivery (liposome, nanoparticle, etc.), and application (gene editing, gene therapy, drug discovery, diagnosis, regulating, and targeting).[95] The 10 main patent holders include the Massachusetts Institute of Technology (MIT), Harvard, Broad Institute, NIH, Sangamo Biosciences, Cellectis, University of California, Dow AgroSciences, DuPont Nutrition Biosciences, and Editas Medicine.

Patent holders, licensors, licensees, and partners are interacting at different levels. The institutional cluster of MIT, the Broad Institute, and Harvard have granted exclusive licenses for therapeutic applications of their CRISPR-Cas technologies to their joint commercial effort, the spin-off company Editas. In addition, they offer academic researchers access through Katz and Pitts 677 Addgene, a nonprofit plasmid repository. UC Berkeley has granted an exclusive license to the startup Caribou Biosciences, which has in turn issued exclusive sublicenses to Intellia and Novartis for therapeutic applications, and to Dupont for agricultural applications. Yet, under pressure from their venture capital backers, these startup companies are aggressively seeking to develop new products of their own and open new markets.

CRISPR may unexpectedly expand its core market to the edition of human reproductive cells. As is already under way with crop seeds, genome editing of human gametes — ova and spermatozoa — could gradually become the next step in CRISPR's industrial application. Initially used by sterile persons and cancer survivors, gamete banks now cater to fertile couples, homosexuals, and one-parent families. Some also market services for young female employees of companies such as Facebook or Apple that offer egg cryopreservation to allow them to build a career while holding off their pregnancy until after age 40.[96]

Polluter Pays
CRISPR could turn this century into a huge wave of genome decontamination. Like the carbon footprint, a genomic footprint disseminated in the general population could be taxed as a prejudice to the common good. CRISPR would make it possible to decontaminate a population's reproductive cells. One could choose not to do so — in the name of individual freedom — but this would spawn a new kind of polluter payer tax, since parents would be taking the risk of disseminating harmful genes in the general population, potentially resulting in costly treatments for the community at large.

Newborn screening programs are an integral part of healthcare policy. In the United States, an analysis of newborn screening in families affected by cystic fibrosis showed that for an average medical cost of $63,127 per year and per patient and an average life span of 37 years, the net savings generated if couples carrying these mutations use IVF and PGD rather than giving birth to a sick child requiring lifelong treatment is estimated at $33.3 billion. Genome editing would multiply these savings, given that IVF with genetic screening only covers one generation, whereas with a single action on the germline, CRISPR would make it possible to modify the DNA of all generations. Through the 20th century, the concept of prevention meant avoiding the appearance of an illness. In the CRISPR century, prevention could come to mean avoiding the appearance of ill persons.

But like other prospective parents, those who rely on donor sperm want to conceive healthy children. The donor selection process gives these parents the opportunity to minimize the risk of recessive disease inheritance by avoiding donors who carry mutations that are genetically incompatible with the reproducing parent. Yet, despite tremendous advances in variant identification, understanding, and analysis, the vast majority of disease-causing mutation combinations remain undetected by commercial carrier screening panels.[97] To overcome this situation, why not use CRISPR directly to commercialize reproductive cells with a customized genome? Today, fertility clinics offer phenotypic details about their sperm donors, from face matching to donor silhouettes, childhood photos, and audio interviews. With CRISPR, they would offer an enhanced genomic quotient to the family and its descendants.

Firms such as GenePeeks and 23andMe have filed patents on technologies that assess the probability of transmitting the genetic diseases of parents to their offspring.[98] The methods for evaluating the genome combinations of two gametes are used to draw up a score that incorporates disease probability, life span, and healthcare expenditures.[99] "I prefer a child with... a low risk of colorectal cancer" is one of the choices in the drop-down menu depicted in 23andMe's patent application.[100] The firm OvaScience is working on an experimental genome-editing technique for oocyte precursor cells that would modify their hereditary predispositions before the embryo is conceived.[101] OvaScience has set up a joint venture with Intrexon, a company specializing in synthetic biology, to accelerate clinical developments in gamete and human embryo genome editing.

The adoption of human germline engineering could be driven by the economic dynamic of supply and demand. Cancer survivors, fertility clinics, biotech firms, oncologists, malpractice insurers, employers, and health authorities are all stakeholders that may find converging interests in the use of germline genome editing, on the individual and collective levels. Figure 2 presents stakeholders' interactions and converging interests in using germline genome editing.

This stakeholder alignment would represent a powerful influence based on an industrial logic rather than an ethical or political consensus. The convergence of economic interests would also be consistent with democratic values such as individual freedom. Indeed, germline modification would represent the freedom of parents to choose the genomic quotient of their offspring at an affordable price, not in the name of "eugenics" but in the name of "hygienics," to prevent genetic pollution and contamination. From this economic perspective, using CRISPR on human germlines could become not only acceptable but also natural and rational.

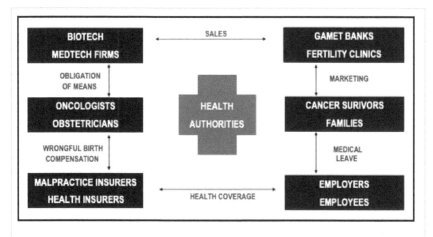

Figure 2: Stakeholder convergence on use of germline genome editing. (i) Cancer survivors could find in CRISPR a way to have children free of cancer predispositions while retaining their fertility capabilities. (ii) Fertility clinics could see in CRISPR a marketing solution that meets the demands of customers looking for reproductive cells with a specific genomic quotient. (iii) Biotech and medtech firms could industrialize their patents by marketing CRISPR to gamete banks and fertility clinics, oncologists, and obstetricians. (iv) Oncologists and obstetricians could use CRISPR to satisfy their obligation of means in order to minimize the risk of transmission of cancer predispositions to the next generation. (v) Malpractice insurers could see CRISPR as a way to avoid wrongful birth claims and costly damages to the families. (vi) Employers offering health insurance to their employees could encourage them to use genome editing to reduce cancer risks that result in medical leaves and healthcare expenditures. (vii) Finally, health authorities could view germline genome editing as a powerful primary prevention tool that would curtail the dissemination of hereditary diseases in the population and decrease healthcare costs.

Voices of Patients

Since the proposal and subsequent confirmation of the structure of DNA, countless bioethical controversies have referred to the concept of "human dignity."[102] But what have we really learned from these debates?[103] That human dignity is a moral value shared by all human beings regardless of their physical characteristics, which includes genetic predispositions. In other words, if CRISPR eliminates a mutation such as KRAS from the human germlines, human dignity will not be diminished. CRISPR children will not be less "human" than children born through IVF or embryo screening. They will be indistinguishable from all other children. They too will be imperfect and lovable. They too will grow, and one day endure disease and eventual death.

The surprising element in the debate over germline modification is the absence of the voices of the patients and their families. Public opinion surveys show that most Americans are in favor of genome editing to prevent their children from inheriting serious diseases,[104] although 65 percent consider that modifying the genes of unborn children should not be legalized.[105] Another survey conducted in 2016 found that 49 percent of Americans approve the use of germline editing to reduce the transmission of hereditary diseases.[106] A caveat to these surveys is that they were conducted in the general population, where cancer survivors statistically represent only a small fraction. In these days of "patient-centricity," it would have been interesting to compare the survey results of the general population with a sample of cancer patients and their families.

"As a parent with an incredibly sick child, what are we supposed to do — sit by on the sidelines while my child dies?… CRISPR is a bullet train that has left the station — there is no stopping it, so how can we harness it for good?"[107] If the proper use of CRISPR should be limited to the "incredibly sick," what criteria should be used to objectively determine these extreme cases? Quality of life? The question is trickier than it may seem. For instance, some consider that autism is a hereditary behavioral trait that is an integral part of human diversity, and that this "neurodiversity" must be respected.[108]

Even before the use of CRISPR on germlines, some people with hereditary deafness or dwarfism were already deciding to selectively transmit those genetic traits to their children in order to share a common way of life.[109] Illness or disability does not necessary imply unhappiness. Several studies show that half the persons with serious diseases consider that their quality of life is good or excellent.[110] In particular, the majority of patients with locked-in syndrome — who can only communicate by blinking their eyes — declare that they are happy despite their state of complete dependence.[111] Why do many people with serious and persistent disabilities report that they experience a good or excellent quality of life when, to most external observers, these people seem to have an undesirable daily experience?[112] The mystery of resilience allows certain diseased persons to overcome the turn of fate, transcend suffering, and create a human endeavor. They succeed "despite," but also "thanks to." Yet with or without resilience, cancer patients will probably refuse to remain passive in the face of illness, forego CRISPR, and let their hereditary predispositions contaminate their descendants.

Concluding Thoughts

Many cancer survivors are quietly consumed by a dilemma: on the one hand, they disapprove of the mass eugenics that would have prevented their own deleterious genomes from coming to life, while on the other hand they wish to benefit from the individual eugenics that would spare their descendants from their own genetic predispositions and suffering. How can these two perspectives be reconciled? More specifically, how can this form of micro-eugenics be condemned when it supports a moral obligation to give our children the best chance of the best life?[113] Yet in a liberal democracy where each individual would be allowed to procreate freely, the cumulative effects of micro-eugenic decisions could eventually lead to macroeugenics bent on favoring the highest genomic quotients. CRISPR could lead to the reemergence of what Nietzsche called "the grand politics [which] places physiology above all other questions — it wants to rear humanity as a whole, it measures the range of the races, of peoples, of individuals according to the guarantee of life that they carry within them. Inexorably it puts an end to everything that is degenerate and parasitical to life."[114] In the CRISPR century, this vision is probably not a prophecy but a possible future.

REFERENCES

1. Nekhulyudov L, Walker R, Ziebell R, Rabin B, Nutt S, Chubak J. Cancer survivors' experiences with insurance, finances, and employment: results from a multisite study. J Cancer Surviv. 2016;10:1104–1111.

2. Alexandrov LB, Nik-Zainal S, Wedge DC, et al. Signatures of mutational processes in human cancer. Nature. 2013;500:415–421.

3. Kandoth C, McLellan MD, Vandin F. Mutational landscape and significance across 12 major

4. Vogelstein B, Papadopoulos N, Velculescu VE, et al. Cancer genome landscapes. Science. 2013;339:1546–1558.

5. Topol E. Individualized medicine from pre-womb to tomb. Cell. 2014;157:241–253.

6. Nakayama T, et al. Simple and efficient CRISPR/Cas9-mediated targeted mutagenesis in Xenopus tropicalis. Genesis. 2013;51:835–843.

7. Doudna J, Charpentier E. The new frontier of genome engineering with CRISPR-Cas9. Science. 2014;346:1258096.

8. Ledford H. Riding the CRISPR wave. Nature. 2016;531:156–159.

9. Hu X, et al. RNA-directed gene editing specifically eradicates latent and prevents new HIV-1 infection. Proc Natl Acad Sci U S A. 2014;111 11461–11466.

10. Hammond A, Galizi R, Kyrou K, et al. A CRISPR-Cas9 gene drive system targeting female reproduction in the malaria mosquito vector Anopheles gambiae. Nat Biotechnol. 2016;34:78–83.

11. Zhang H, Zhang J, Wei P, et al. The CRISPR/Cas9 system produces specific and homozygous targeted gene editing in rice in one generation. Plant Biotechnol J. 2014;12:797–807.

12. Jia H, Wang N. Targeted genome editing of sweet orange using Cas9/sgRNA. PLoS One. 2014;9:e93806.

13. Wang Z. Genome engineering in cattle: recent technological advancements. Chromosome Res. 2015;23:17–29.

14. Reardon S. The CRISPR zoo. Nature. 2016;531:160–163.

15. Shi J, Wang E, Milazzo JP, et al. Discovery of cancer drug targets by CRISPR-Cas9 screening of protein domains. Nat Biotechnol. 2015;33:661–667.

16. Yin H, Xue W, Chen S, et al. Genome editing with Cas9 in adult mice corrects a disease mutation and phenotype. Nat Biotechnol. 2014;32:551–553.

17. Long C, McAnally JR, Shelton JM, et al. Prevention of muscular dystrophy in mice by CRISPR/Cas9-mediated editing of germline DNA. Science. 2014;345:1184–1188.

18. Li HL, Fujimoto N, Sasakawa N, Shirai S, Ohkame T, Sakuma T. Precise correction of the dystrophin gene in Duchenne muscular dystrophy patient induced pluripotent stem cells by TALEN and CRISPR-Cas9. Stem Cell Rep. 2015;4:143–154.

19. Tabebordbar M, Zhu K, Cheng JKW, et al. In vivo gene editing in dystrophic mouse muscle and muscle stem cells. Science. 2016;351:407–411.

20. Wu Y, Liang D, Wang Y, et al. Correction of a genetic disease in mouse via use of CRISPR-Cas9. Cell Stem Cell. 2013;13:659–662.

21. Chen J-R, Tang ZH, Zheng J, et al. Effects of genetic correction on the differentiation of hair cell-like cells from iPSCs with MYO15A mutation. Cell Death Differ. 2016;23:1347–1357.

22. Xie F, Tang ZH, Zheng J, et al. Genome editing with Cas9 in adult mice corrects a disease mutation and phenotype. Nat Biotechnol. 2014;32:551–553.

23. Shalem O, Sanjana NE, Hartenian E, et al. Genome-scale CRISPR-Cas9 knockout screening in human cells. Science. 2014;343:84–87.

24. Schwank G, Koo BK, Sasselli V, et al. Functional repair of CFTR by CRISPR/Cas9 in intestinal cell organoids of cystic fibrosis patients. Cell Stem Cell. 2013;13:653–658.

25. Reardon S. Gene editing wave hits clinic. Nature. 2015;527:146–147.

26. Cyranoski D. First trial of CRISPR in people. Nature. 2016;535:476–477.

27. Kaiser J. First proposed human test of CRISPR passes initial safety review. Science, June 21, 2016.

28. Mulder C, Zheng Y, Jan SZ, et al. Spermatogonial stem cell autotransplantation and germline genomic editing: a future cure for spermatogenic failure and prevention of transmission of genomic diseases. Hum Reprod Update. 2016;5:561–573.

29. Chapman KM, Medrano GA, Jaichander P, et al. Targeted germline modifications in rats using CRISPR/Cas9 and spermatogonial stem cells. Cell Rep. 2015;10:1828–1835.

30. Sato T, Sakuma T, Yokonishi T, et al. Genome editing in mouse spermatogonial stem cell lines using TALEN and double-nicking CRISPR/Cas9. Stem Cell Rep. 2015;5:75–82.

31. Vassena R, Heindryckx B, Peco R, et al. Genome engineering through CRISPR/Cas9 technology in the human germline and pluripotent stem cells. Hum Reprod Update. 2016;22:411–419.

32. Gomy I, Del Pilar Estevez Diz M. Hereditary cancer risk assessment: insights and perspectives for Next-Generation Sequencing era. Genet Mol Biol. 2016;39:184–188.

33. Kraus C, Rau T, Lux P, et al. Comprehensive screening for mutations associated with colorectal cancer in unselected cases reveals penetrant and nonpenetrant mutations. Int J Cancer. 2015;136:E559–E568.

34. Nelson HD, Fu R, Goddard K, et al. Risk Assessment, Genetic Counseling, and Genetic Testing for BRCA-Related Cancer: Systematic Review to Update the U.S. Preventive Services Task Force Recommendation. Evidence Syntheses, No. 101. Rockville, MD: US Agency for Healthcare Research and Quality; 2013.

35. Pharoah PD, Antoniou A, Bobrow M, et al. Polygenic susceptibility to breast cancer and implications for prevention. Nat Genet. 2002;31:33–36.

36. Houlston RS, Peto F. The search for low-penetrance cancer susceptibility alleles. Oncogene. 2004;23:6471–6476.

37. Newson A, Leonard S, Hall A, Gaff CL. Known unknowns: building an ethics of uncertainty into genomic medicine. BMC Med Genom. 2016;9:57.

38. Robson ME, Bradbury AR, Arun B, et al. American Society of Clinical Oncology policy statement update: genetic and genomic testing for cancer susceptibility. J Clin Oncol. 2015;33:3660–3667.

39. Lynce F, Isaacs C. How Far Do We Go With Genetic Evaluation? Gene, Panel, and Tumor Testing. ASCO Educational Book. 2016;E72.

40. Kaiser J, Normile D. Embryo engineering study splits scientific community. Science. 2015;348:486–487.

41. Araki M, Ishii T. International regulatory landscape and integration of corrective genome editing into in vitro fertilization. Reprod Biol Endocrinol. 2014;12:108.

42. UNESCO. http://www.unesco.org/new/en/social-and-human-sciences/themes/bioethics/sv0/news/unesco_panel_of_experts_calls_for_ban_on_editing_of_human_dna_to_avoid_unethical_tampering_with_hereditary_traits/#.VwgJUvkrJaQ. 2015.

43. Ledford H. The landscape for human genome editing. Nature. 2015;526:310–311.

44. Council of Europe, Convention on Human Rights and Biomedecine, article 13. https://rm.coe.int/CoERMPublicCommonSearchServices/DisplayDCTMContent?documentId=090000168049034a (2015).

45. The Human Fertilisation and Embryology (Mitochondrial Donation) Regulations 2015 No. 572. http://www.legislation.gov.uk/ukdsi/2015/9780111125816/contents.

46. Liang P, Xu Y, Zhang X, et al. CRISPR/Cas9-mediated gene editing in human tripronuclear zygotes. Protein Cell. 2015;6:363–372.

47. The National Academies of Science, Engineering and Medicine. International Summit on Human Gene Editing. http://www8.nationalacademies.org/onpinews/newsitem.aspx?RecordID=12032015a. Published December 3, 2015.

48. Reardon S. Global summit reveals divergent views on human gene editing. Nature. 2015;528:173.

49. Collins FS. Statement on NIH funding of research using gene-editing technologies in human embryos. National Institutes of Health. https://www.nih.gov/about-nih/who-we-are/nih-director/statements/statement-nih-funding-research-using-gene-editing-technologies-human-embryos. Published 2015.

50. DiCarlo JE, Chavez A, Dietz SL, Esvelt KM, Church GM. Safeguarding CRISPR-Cas9 gene drives in yeast. Nat Biotechnol. 2015;33:1250–1255.

51. Akbari OS, Bellen HJ, Bier E, et al. Biosafety. Safeguarding gene drive experiments in the laboratory. Science. 2015;349:927–929.

52. Newson AJ, Wrigley A. Identifying key developments, issues and questions relating to techniques of genome editing with engineered nucleases. Background paper. London: Nuffield Council on Bioethics. http://nuffieldbioethics.org/wp-content/uploads/Genome-Editing-Briefing-Paper-Newson-Wrigley.pdf (2015).

53. Brice P. First UK birth following PGD for hereditary breast cancer PHG Foundation, January 9, 2009. http://www.phgfoundation.org/news/4445/. Published 2016.

54. Gelbaya TA. Short and long-term risks to women who conceive through in vitro fertilization. Hum Fertil. 2010;13:19–27.

55. Hansen M, Kurinczuk JJ, Milne E, de Klerk N, Bower C. Assisted reproductive technology and birth defects: a systematic review and meta-analysis. Hum Reprod Update. 2013;19:330–353.

56. Kaimal A, Norton M, Kuppermann M. Prenatal testing in the genomic age: clinical outcomes, quality of life and costs. Obstet Gynecol. 2015;126:737–746.

57. Verhoef TI, Hill M, Drury S. Non-invasive prenatal diagnosis (NIPD) for single gene disorders: cost analysis of NIPD and invasive testing pathways. Prenat Diagn. 2016;36:636–642.

58. Benett J, Chitty L, Lewis C. Non-invasive prenatal diagnosis for BRCA mutations — a qualitative pilot study of health professionals' views. J Genet Counsel. 2016;25:198–207.

59. Ramsey S, Blough D, Kirchhoff A, et al. Washington State cancer patients found to be at greater risk for bankruptcy than people without a cancer diagnosis. Health Aff. 2013;32:1143–1152.

60. Fenn KM, Evans SB, McCorkle R, et al. Impact of financial burden of cancer on survivors' quality of life. J Oncol Pract. 2014;10:332–338.

61. deBoer AG, Taskila T, Ojajärvi A, van Dijk FJ, Verbeek JH. Cancer survivors and unemployment: a meta-analysis and meta-regression. JAMA. 2009;301:753–762.

62. Guy GP Jr., Ekwueme DU, Yabroff KR, et al. Economic burden of cancer survivorship among adults in the United States. J Clin Oncol. 2013;31:3749–3957.

63. Yabroff KR, Dowling EC, Guy GP Jr., et al. Financial hardship associated with cancer in the United States: findings from a population-based sample of adult cancer survivors. J Clin Oncol. 2016;34:259–267.

64. Lathan CS, Cronin A, Tucker-Seeley R, Zafar SY, Ayanian JZ, Schrag D. Association of financial strain with symptom burden and quality of life for patients with lung or colorectal cancer. J Clin Oncol. 2016;34:1732–1740.

65. Kale HP, Carroll NV. Self-reported financial burden of cancer care and its effect on physical and mental health-related quality of life among US cancer survivors. Cancer. 2016;122:238–239.

66. Ramsey SD, Bansal A, Fedorenko CR, et al. Financial insolvency as a risk factor for early mortality among patients with cancer. J Clin Oncol. 2016;34:980–986.

67. NIH, National Cancer Institute. Cancer prevalence and cost of care projections. https://costprojections.cancer.gov/expenditures.html#. Published 2016.

68. Luengo-Fernandez R, Leal J, Gray A, Sullivan R. Economic burden of cancer across the European Union: a population-based cost analysis. Lancet Oncol. 2013;14:1165–1174.

69. Lyman G. Counting the costs of cancer care. Lancet Oncol. 2013;14:1142–1143.

70. Tefferi A, Kantarjian H, Rajkumar V, et al. In support of a patient-driven initiative and petition to lower the high price of cancer drugs. Mayo Clin Proc. 2015;90:996–1000.

71. US Census Bureau. Families and households. http://www.census.gov/hhes/families/index.html. Accessed January 1, 2017.

72. McCarthy M. US oncologists call for government regulation to curb drug price rises. BMJ. 2015;351:h4063.

73. NIH, National Human Genome Research Institute. DNA Sequencing Costs: Data. https://www.genome.gov/27541954/dna-sequencing-costs-data/dna-sequencing-costs-data/. Accessed January 1, 2017.

74. ThermoFisher Scientific. GeneArt Platinum Cas9 Nuclease & Lipofectamine CRISPRMAX. https://www.thermofisher.com/fr/fr/home/life-science/genome-editing/geneart-crispr/crispr-protein.html. Accessed January 1, 2017.

75. Boettcher M, McManus M. Choosing the right tool for the job: RNAi, TALEN, or CRISPR. Mol Cell. 2015;58:575–585.

76. Unniyampurath U, Pilankatta R, Krishnan M. RNA interference in the age of CRISPR: will CRISPR interfere with RNAi? Int J Mol Sci. 2016;17:291.

77. Schumpeter JA. Capitalism, Socialism and Democracy. London: Routledge; 1942:82–83.

78. Subramanian S, Tangka FK, Hoover S, et al., Recommendations from the international colorectal cancer screening network on the evaluation of the cost of screening programs. J Public Health Manag Pract. 2015;22:461–465.

79. Ouakrim D, Boussioutas A, Lockett T, Hopper JL, Jenkins MA. Cost-effectiveness of family history-based colorectal cancer screening in Australia. BMC Cancer. 2014;14:261.

80. Pil L, Fobelets M, Putman K, et al. Cost-effectiveness and budget impact analysis of a population-based screening program for colorectal cancer. Eur J Int Med. 2016;32:72–78.

81. President's Council of Advisors on Science and Technology. Priorities for Personalized Medicine. Office of Science and Technology, US, 2008. https://www.whitehouse.gov/files/documents/ostp/PCAST/pcast_report_v2.pdf.

82. Towse A, Garrison L. Value Assessment in Precision Cancer Medicine. J Cancer Policy. 2016. https://doi.org/10.1016/j.jcpo.2016.09.003.

83. Harris L, Ismaila N, McShane LM, et al. Use of biomarkers to guide decisions on adjuvant systemic therapy for women with early-stage invasive breast cancer: American Society of Clinical Oncology Clinical Practice Guideline. J Clin Oncol. 2016;34:1134–1150.

84. National Institute for Health and Care Excellence. Gene expression profiling and expanded immunohistochemistry tests for guiding adjuvant chemotherapy decisions in early breast cancer management: MammaPrint, Oncotype DX, IHC4 and Mammostrat. https://www.nice.org.uk/guidance/DG10. Accessed January 1, 2017.

85. Katz G, Romano O, Foa C, et al. Economic impact of gene expression profiling in patients with early-stage breast cancer in France. PLoS One. 2015;10:1–15.

86. Lander E. Brave new genome. N Engl J Med. 2015;373:1.

87. Katz G, Schweitzer S. Implications of genetic testing for health policy. Yale J Health Policy Law Ethics. 2010;10:89–134.

88. Joly Y, Burton H, Knoppers BM, et al. Life Insurance: genomic stratification and risk classification. Eur J Hum Genet. 2014;22:575–579.

89. Withrock I, Anderson S, Jefferson M, et al. Genetic diseases conferring resistance to infectious diseases. Genes Dis. 2015;2:247–254.

90. Quételet A. Anthropométrie ou mesure des différentes facultés de l'homme (1870), Nabu Press, 2014.

91. Macdonald AS. Genetic factors in life insurance. Actuarial basis. In: Encyclopedia of Life Science. Chichester, UK: Wiley; 2009.

92. Van Hoyweghen I, Rebert L. Your genes in insurance: from genetic discrimination to genomics solidarity. Pers Med. 2012;9:871–877.

93. Van Erp PBG, Bloomer G, Wilkinson R, Wiedenheft B. The history and market impact of CRISPR RNA-guided nucleases. Curr Opin Virol. 2015;12:85–90.

94. Editing Humanity. The Economist, August 22–28, 2015.

95. Egelie K, Graff G, Strand S, Johansen B. The emerging patent landscape of CRISPR-Cas gene editing technology. Nat Biotechnol. 2016;34:1025–1031.

96. Zoll M, Mertes H, Gupta J, Corporate giants provide fertility benefits: have they got it wrong? Eur J Obstet Gynecol Reprod Biol. 2015;195:A1–A2.

97. Silver AJ, Larson JL, Silver MJ. Carrier screening is a deficient strategy for determining sperm donor eligibility and reducing risk of disease in recipient children. Genet Test Mol Biomarkers. 2016;20:276–284.

98. Rojahn Y. Genetic screening can uncover risky matches at the sperm bank. MIT Technology Review, November 20, 2012.

99. Wojcicki A, Avey L, Mountain JL, McPherson JM, Tung JYH. Gamete donor selection based on genetic calculations. US 2010/0145981 A1, paria. [0014]. 2010. US Patent and Trademark Office. Notice of Allowance in Relation to US Patent Application Serial No. 12/592950.

100. Sterckx S, Cockbain J, Howard H, Borry P. «I prefer a child with…»: designer babies, another controversial patent in the arena of direct-to-consumer genomics. Genet Med. 2013;15:923–924.

101. Regalado A. Engineering the perfect baby. MIT Technology Review, March 5, 2015.

102. Hildt E. Human germline intervention — think first. Front Genet. 2016;7:81.

103. Sugarman J. Ethics and germline gene editing, EMBO Rep. 2015;16:879–880.

104. Blendon R, et al. The public and the gene-editing revolution. N Eng J Med. 2016;374:1406–1411.

105. STAT-Harvard T.H. Chan School of Public Health. The public and genetic editing, testing and therapy. https://cdn1.sph.harvard.edu/wp-content/uploads/sites/94/2016/01/STAT-Harvard-Poll-Jan-2016-Genetic-Technology.pdf (2016).

106. Pew Research Center. US public wary of biomedical technologies to "enhance" human abilities, July 26, 2016. http://www.pewinternet.org/2016/07/26/u-s-public-wary-of-biomedical-technologies-to-enhance-human-abilities/.

107. Hayden EC. Tomorrow's children. Nature. 2016;530:402–405.

108. Hayden EC. Tomorrow's children. Nature. 2016;530:402–405.

109. Häyry M. There is a difference between selecting a deaf embryo and deafening a hearing child. J Med Ethics. 2004;30:510–512.

110. Albrecht GL, Devlieger PJ. The disability paradox: high quality of life against all odds. Soc Sci Med. 1999;48:977–988.

111. Bruno MA. A survey on self-assessed well-being in a cohort of chronic locked-in syndrome patients: happy majority, miserable minority. BMJ Open. 2011;1:e000039.

112. Levine S. The changing terrains in medical sociology: emergent concern with the quality of life. J Health Soc Behav. 1987;28:1–6.

113. Savulescu J, Kahane G. The moral obligation to create children with the best chance of the best life. Bioethics. 2009;23:274–290.

114. Nietzsche, Fragments posthumes 1888–1889, JC, tome XIV, Oeuvres philosophiques complètes, trad. Hemery, Paris, Gallimard (1977).

The Privacy Delusions of Genetic Testing

By Peter J. Pitts

Originally published in *Forbes*, February 15, 2017

Genetic testing promises a revolution in healthcare. With just a few swabs of saliva, diagnostics can provide an unprecedented look into a person's family history and potential health risks. Within a decade, global sales of genetic tests are expected to hit $10 billion. Direct-to-consumer companies such as 23andMe and Genos have proven particularly popular, with tens of thousands of people purchasing at-home testing kits every year.

But the industry's rapid growth rests on a dangerous delusion: that genetic data is kept private. Most people assume this sensitive information simply sits in a secure database, protected from hacks and misuse.

Far from it. Genetic-testing companies cannot guarantee privacy. And many are actively selling user data to outside parties.

The problem starts with the Health Insurance Portability and Accountability Act (HIPAA), a 1996 federal law that allows medical companies to share and sell patient data if it has been "anonymized," or scrubbed of any obvious identifying characteristics.

The Portability Act was passed when genetic testing was just a distant dream on the horizon of personalized medicine. But today, that loophole has proven to be a cash cow. For instance, 23andMe has sold access to its database to at least 13 outside pharmaceutical firms. One buyer, Genentech, ponied up a cool $10 million for the genetic profiles of people suffering from Parkinson's. AncestryDNA, another popular personal genetics company, recently announced a lucrative data-sharing partnership with the biotech company Calico.

Customers are wrong to think their information is safely locked away. It's not; it's getting sold far and wide. Many testing firms that generally don't sell patient information, such as Ambry and Invitae, give it away to public databases. Such transfers, as privacy consultant Bob Gellman puts it, leave a "big gap in protections." Hacks are inevitable. Easily accessible, public genetic depositories are obvious targets.

If genetic data does fall into the hands of nefarious actors, it's relatively easy for them to de-anonymize it. New lab techniques can unearth genetic markers tied to specific, physical traits, such as eye or hair color. Sleuths can then cross-reference those traits against publicly available demographic data to identify the donors.

Using this process, one MIT scientist was able to identify the people behind five supposedly anonymous genetic samples randomly selected from a public research database. It took him less than a day. Likewise, a Harvard Medical School professor dug up the identities of over 80 percent of the samples housed in his school's genetic database. Privacy protections can be broken. Indeed, no less than Linda Avey, a cofounder of 23andMe, has explicitly admitted that "it's a fallacy to think that genomic data can be fully anonymized."

Once genetic data has been linked to a specific person, the potential for abuse is vast and frightening. Imagine a political campaign exposing a rival's elevated risk of Alzheimer's. Or an employer refusing to hire someone because autism runs in her family. Imagine a world where people can have their biology held against them. Such abuses represent a profound violation of privacy. That's the risk inherent in current genetic-testing practices.

For their part, direct-to-consumer testing companies have been less than forthright about these dangers, usually burying privacy disclaimers deep in their contracts and refusing to disclose how long they keep customer data or how it can be used.

23andMe customers have to wade through pages of fine print before finding out that their information may be "shared with research partners, including commercial partners." AncestryDNA's contract claims a "perpetual, royalty-free, worldwide, transferable license to use your DNA." New research published in the journal *Nature* found that genetic-testing companies frequently fail to meet even basic international transparency standards.

Genetic testing has tremendous benefits. We are provided a closer look at our own biology. Medical researchers develop a deeper understanding of the origins of disease and can create powerful new treatments. But today, far too many donors are operating under a false sense of security, handling profoundly intimate data without appropriate protections.

The Lessons of COVID-19

"We can draw lessons from the past, but we cannot live in it." LYNDON JOHNSON

Believe it or not, there are urgent healthcare issues that are not exclusively pandemic-specific. As we move forward, our thinking, planning, and execution of a whole host of healthcare opportunities must be informed by the tough and valuable lessons we have learned (but are still largely ignoring) from our battle against COVID-19. Hindsight is 20/20. If there's one thing we cannot afford to forget or minimize from our fight against COVID-19, it's the value of preparation. Aristotle reminds us, "Excellence is never an accident. It is always the result of high intention, sincere effort, and intelligent execution; it represents the wise choice of many alternatives."

Healthcare Lessons Ignored from Our Fight Against COVID-19

By Peter J. Pitts

Originally published in *The Washington Times*, February 13, 2021

Believe it or not, there are urgent healthcare issues facing our nation that are not exclusively pandemic-specific. As we move forward with a new administration in Washington, our thinking, planning, and execution of a whole host of healthcare opportunities must be informed by the tough and valuable lessons we have learned (but are still largely ignoring) from our battle against COVID-19.

1. The Urgency of Coordination

The current problems we're dealing with relative to vaccine roll-out remind us how much we have learned — and how little we have absorbed. If, in March of 2020, I had predicted we'd have a well-stocked COVID-19 armamentarium replete with diagnostics, therapeutics, and vaccines by the end of the year — I would have been accused of wishful thinking.

COVID-19 Urgency Lesson #1:

If we learn nothing else from our pandemic experience, it's that a key facilitator of velocity is broad participation. We can accomplish great things quickly when we work together. Our healthcare ecosystem, including the biopharmaceutical industry, academia, government health agencies, manufacturing logicians, hospitalists, healthcare workers, pharmacists, patients, and caregivers all helped to accelerate our understanding of the virus, how to mitigate it, flatten the curve, and save lives. Imagine what we will accomplish working together more regularly on a wide array of opportunities to improve the human condition? This is as relevant for COVID-19 as it is for the further development of the patient voice in drug development.

2. The Urgency of Innovation

Medical science has consistently found new ways to extend and improve lives. Wonderful as they are, they do not come cheap. Shortly before his death, I had the privilege of a private meeting with Nobel laureate Joshua Lederberg. We talked about the state of applied science, the prioritization of development science, biomarkers, and a host of other future-oriented issues. At the end of the meeting he put everything into perspective in a single sentence. He leaned over the table and said, "The real question should be, is innovation feasible?" Our pandemic experience proves that it is. But there are many issues beyond those of discovery and development. The complicated and conflicting dynamics of politics, perspectives on healthcare economics, of friction between payers, providers, manufacturers, and regulators, the battle for better patient education, and the need for a more forceful and factual debate over the value of innovation all create the need for a more balanced and robust debate.

COVID-19 Urgency Lesson #2:
Innovation is never as easy as it looks. Consider the imbroglio over convalescent plasma, clinical trial design, and data collection. The reality is that innovation takes time. As any scientist will tell you, innovation happens step by step, one incremental innovation at a time. Innovation is hard. It takes about 10,000 new molecules to produce one FDA-approved medicine. Nonetheless, innovation is important. Beyond COVID-19, we must also embrace innovative technologies for medical records and prescribing. We need innovative clinical trial designs and molecular diagnostics so that we can develop better, more personalized medicines faster and for far less than the current $1 billion-plus delivery charge. We need innovation in access and reimbursement policies that rewards speed to best treatment rather than lower-cost patients per hour.

3. The Urgency of 21st-Century FDA Regulatory Policy
Be honest, before COVID-19, did you even know what an Emergency Use Authorization was? To address urgent needs, the FDA issued EUAs for diagnostics, therapeutics, and vaccines. How was this possible? It's thanks to advances in regulatory science. Alas, the status quo is a harsh mistress. Too many people want to go back to the way things were. But there's no turning back. While scientifically robust standards and practices are the twin underpinnings of regulatory science, they are by no stretch of the imagination etched in twin tablets by divine fire. Such an antiquated attitude only leads to a diminished desire to invest in innovation. The most potent way medicines regulators can enable innovation is by being a partner in advancing new approaches to both drug development and regulatory science. That also means a more three-dimensional view of "safety." What does "safety" mean? How is it measured? What is its role in the benefit/risk proposition? Who is its arbiter and guardian? What are the ground rules? What are the pitfalls and opportunities presented by new technologies? Posing the tough questions is a crucial first step.

COVID-19 Urgency Lesson #3:
The FDA can either be a sea anchor to or an accelerator of innovation. Change is uncomfortable. A universal truth from human behavioral science is that those doing the work are uncomfortable when the ground rules change. According to Rosabeth Moss Kanter of Harvard Business School, "The best tool for leaders of change is to understand the predictable,

universal sources of resistance in each situation and then strategize around them." The good news is that the FDA recognizes it must be a leader in regulatory science — the science of developing new tools, standards, and approaches to assess the safety, efficacy, quality, and performance of all FDA-regulated products — by dint of true expertise rather than for simply "being the FDA." COVID-19 has reinforced the FDA's understanding that laying claim to the regulatory gold standard is a moving target.

4. The Urgency of Science

On November 17, 1944, President Franklin Roosevelt wrote to Vannevar Bush, the director of the three-year-old Office of Scientific Research and Development, "New frontiers of the mind are before us, and if they are pioneered with the same vision, boldness, and drive with which we have waged this war we can create a fuller and more fruitful employment and a fuller and more fruitful life." As Bush responded to the president in his 1945 report, "Science: The Endless Frontier": "Science can be effective in the national welfare only as a member of a team, whether the conditions be peace or war. But without scientific progress no amount of achievement in other directions can insure our health, prosperity, and security as a nation in the modern world." When it comes to healthcare writ large and regulated healthcare technologies specifically, quality is a sine qua non. We've learned a lot from COVID-19. How are we going to share that knowledge and maximize it to the fullest potential?

COVID-19 Urgency Lesson #4:

Without science, nothing happens. Science must not be silenced or siloed. Science must be collegial, intramural, and transnational. Science can be expedited but not rushed. Science cannot be politicized. And science must be trusted by all constituencies from highly degreed academics and regulators to family doctors and patients. Trust counts. We need not look any further than the fact that so many Americans do not trust the FDA process sufficiently to get vaccinated against COVID-19.

5. The Urgency of Preparation

When it comes to placing blame for the devastation of COVID-19, laying it all at the feet of Donald Trump is facile and dangerous. We were as a nation, unwilling, unable, and unprepared. This must never happen again.

COVID-19 Urgency Lesson #5: Be Prepared.

They say hindsight is 20/20, and if there's one thing we take away from our fight against COVID-19, it's the value of preparation. We need:

A fully independent sustaining infrastructure for disaster preparedness and oversight.

A renewed commitment to national approaches for all microbial threats, foreign and domestic — and the means and methodologies to support all states, ensuring that the necessary tools and capabilities are readily available on a real-time basis.

A singular national source of authoritative advice that represents the consensus of best thinking and practices from clinicians, epidemiologists, allied health professionals and political entities — with the tacit agreement to always default to public health interests and truthful transparency.

An active engagement in global risk monitoring and data-sharing networks, to more rapidly detect and address these threats.

Improved development approaches via collaborative endeavors that fully adhere to rigorous scientific standards; our battle against COVID-19 will be judged by history, but a brutally honest and introspective analysis of our current successes and failures must act as a roadmap to protect future generations of Americans.

Aristotle reminds us, "Excellence is never an accident. It is always the result of high intention, sincere effort, and intelligent execution; it represents the wise choice of many alternatives. Choice, not chance, determines your destiny." Nobody said it was going to be easy.

Vaccine Hesitancy: When Political Miscommunication Replaces Scientific Benefit/Risk Assessment

By Christian Rausch, Peter J. Pitts, and Hervé le Louët

Originally published in the *Journal of Commercial Biotechnology*, December 2021

Around the world, scientists, manufacturers, and governments jumped into the race to develop a vaccine to combat COVID-19 and its associated lockdowns. A global response was required since defeating the pandemic requires global alignment. The availability of COVID-19 vaccines has always been a major concern for the WHO particularly in low- and middle-income countries. While the vaccine development programs vaccination moved successfully forward, another problem, vaccine hesitancy, became a worrying factor in the movement toward herd immunity in many countries. Several factors contribute to this predicament.[1]

First, there is confusion between *vaccines* and *vaccinations*. Many people refuse to accept "mandated" vaccination, because they consider their health decisions to be a personal choice and a matter of individual dignity. Government mandates have revealed a deep disconnection between the government and society. The problem is not exclusively the safety and efficacy of any one vaccine *per se*, but a backlash against a public health intervention that is viewed as coercive.

Experts give their informed, evidence-based opinions on vaccines, yet vaccination programs are political decisions made in consideration of national and global public health perspectives. The decision to recommend and/or mandate vaccination is not only a benefit/risk assessment but also factors in societal, economic, and other related issues deemed important by political leadership. These non-health-related factors are complex and difficult to explain to the general population as they rely on information and interests from different areas of society and are not always immediately clear in their motivations and broader purposes.

Second is the ability of national, regional, and global pharmacovigilance (PV) systems to provide a clear and united vision of the efficiency and safety of COVID-19 vaccines. Currently PV systems are oriented to the detection, via large databases, of side effects using automatic signal detection based on statistical disproportionality, resulting in the identification of short-term, high-level clinical events. However, in some cases the clinical relevance and the broader public health impact is unclear. "Black Swan" clinical events can easily be taken out of context and misused and manipulated for other purposes in various media platforms like social media. Other tools like pharmacoepidemiologic studies should be promptly implemented in order to provide a nuanced and realistic vision of reality. The use of pharmacoepidemiologic tools is needed in more local settings as well to accurately assess the impact of Black Swan–like signals in specific national and regional contexts. "Detailing the facts" will aid in both developing and optimizing the local response and communications.

We believe that miscommunication is a major component of global vaccine hesitancy for many reasons. The spread of misinformation plays a dangerous role, particularly as anti-vaccination campaigns play politics with the public health and magnify the mistrust of many people.[2] The appearance of rare unforeseen side effects, like thrombotic events, are disproportionally magnified by the media, raising undue public concern. Appropriate due diligence of all side effects are needed, but so is a clear communication of the data and facts available from trustworthy organizations with little delay.[3,4] This can only be done in partnership with public health authorities, healthcare providers, and the media. Lack of a consolidated and coordinated reaction to an identified Black Swan event and its legitimate place in the benefit/risk analysis hampers the successful implementation of vaccination strategies. Inconsistency, lack of proportionality and lack of clarity in the communication of available facts must be urgently avoided.

These issues are not unique to low-and-middle-income nations. As such, global cooperation is the order of the day. Ecosystem problems require ecosystem solutions. The real formula is well known — dedication and a lot of effort from healthcare professionals, patients, academicians, transnational organizations, and, yes — even politicians from every corner of the globe. Easy to articulate but difficult to implement.

A "one-size-fits-all" strategy, where the impact of any individual signal is considered relevant for all contexts, is no longer valid or productive. Communications measures should be aimed at protecting and supporting the trust of the public and ensure that a problem like vaccine hesitancy cannot derail efforts to defeat a global pandemic — where every jab counts.

REFERENCES:

1. Solís Arce JS, Warren SS, Meriggi NF, et al. COVID-19 vaccine acceptance and hesitancy in low- and middle-income countries. Nat Med. Published online July 16, 2021:1–10. doi:10.1038/s41591-021-01454-y.

2. Loomba S, de Figueiredo A, Piatek SJ, de Graaf K, Larson HJ. Measuring the impact of COVID-19 vaccine misinformation on vaccination intent in the UK and USA. Nat Hum Behav. 2021;5(3):337–348. doi:10.1038/s41562-021-01056-1.

3. Kerr JR, Freeman ALJ, Marteau TM, van der Linden S. Effect of Information about COVID-19 Vaccine Effectiveness and Side Effects on Behavioural Intentions: Two Online Experiments. Vaccines (Basel). 2021;9(4):379. doi:10.3390/vaccines9040379.

4. Remmel A. 'It's a minefield': COVID vaccine safety poses unique communication challenge. Nature. 2021;593(7860):488–489. doi:10.1038/d41586-021-01257-8.

The Other Vaccine Denial

By Peter J. Pitts

Originally published in *RealClearHealth*, July 28, 2021

There's another insidious kind of vaccine denial — denial of coverage. The good news is there's a piece of pending bipartisan legislation to address it. HR 1978, The Protecting Seniors Through Immunization Act, would eliminate out-of-pocket costs for vaccines covered under Medicare Part D and improves vaccine awareness and education for beneficiaries.

Some background: In the US we spend about $26.5 billion annually treating four major vaccine-preventable diseases among US adults (flu, pneumococcal, shingles, pertussis). Vaccines covered under Medicare Part D — such as tetanus, diphtheria, and pertussis (Tdap) and shingles — require varying levels of out-of-pocket costs for patients that can reduce acceptance of vaccines and therefore affect vaccine rates. By contrast, vaccines covered under Medicare Part B — such as flu and pneumococcal — require *no* out-of-pocket costs from patients, leading to higher vaccination rates.

Beyond these four major vaccines, there are additional important public health imperatives addressed by HR 1978:

COVID-19: A component of combatting COVID-19 is a wider adoption of preventive health strategies to reduce the burden of co-morbid conditions that put people at higher risk of worse outcomes of COVID-19. Immunizing indicated populations against non-COVID-19 vaccine-preventable diseases (VPD) will both contribute to better health outcomes overall and preserve vital capacity at hospitals by reducing preventable admissions.

Pandemic Preparedness: The COVID-19 pandemic demonstrated all too clearly how important vaccines are to both the physical and economic health and well-being of Americans. And our seniors suffered greatly from this disease. We need to ensure that Medicare beneficiaries never face financial barriers to getting vaccinated, whether it's for an infectious disease that caused a global pandemic or any other debilitating or life-threatening condition. Congress should permanently eliminate all cost sharing for vaccines in Medicare D to ensure seniors don't face financial barriers to getting lifesaving preventive services.

Highlighting Appropriate Utilization and Building Confidence: The stated goal of cost sharing is to reduce inappropriate healthcare utilization. Immunization has health benefits for both the individual and for society and should be incented, not discouraged. By waiving the cost share, Congress recognizes and signal that vaccines are a safe and effective tool in public health. As more people become immunized, the practice becomes more ensconced in the community as part of preventive health.

Reducing Hospital Burden: Reducing unnecessary hospitalizations by increasing access to Part D vaccines will reduce hospitalizations. Vaccines in development can reduce hospital burden even further. For example, in the future, immunizing Medicare Part D beneficiaries against Clostridioides difficile (C. diff) and respiratory syncytial virus (RSV) would reduce the diversion of hospital resources dedicated to responding to these infections and in the case of C. diff, eliminate a hospital-acquired condition to which Medicare assigns financial penalties and C. diff and RSV vaccines also represent immunizations against conditions that would otherwise be treated with antibiotics. Preventing infection through immunization contributes to the national effort to combat antimicrobial resistance.

Beyond COVID-19, a fully vaccinated public is an investment in the health, well-being, and economic success of our nation.

Speaking to/Through America's Newspaper of Record

"Please give me some good advice in your next letter. I promise not to follow it."

EDNA ST. VINCENT MILLAY

As the saying goes, "everything you read about in the newspaper is true — except for those things you know about personally." Nowhere is this truer, more important, or more frustrating than when it comes to our nation's newspaper of record, *The New York Times*, and how the Gray Lady reports on healthcare policy issues. "Highly respected and widely quoted" isn't (alas) always synonymous with accurate, judicious, or objective. Oftentimes the only recourse is to write a response and hope it gets published. When a letter or commentary does get published, it helps to both set the record straight and refocus the conversation.

Healthcare and Reality

Originally published in *The New York Times*, August 14, 2008

To the Editor:

Re "Can It Happen Here?" (column, August 11):

Paul Krugman states that "in principle, it should be easy" for the Democrats to deliver on their promise to "provide every American access to affordable, comprehensive health care."

It sure hasn't been easy for the countries that have tried.

In Canada, according to the Fraser Institute, patients seeking specialized treatment had to wait 18.3 weeks in 2007. Approximately 875,000 Canadians are on waiting lists for treatment.

A 1997 study in *Health Policy* found that whereas the average wait time for bypass surgery in New York State was 17 days, it was 72 days in the Netherlands and 59 days in Sweden.

In Britain, the government's cost-effectiveness agency just announced that patients can't rely on the National Health Service to save their lives if the cost of doing so is too high.

This is the reality in government-run healthcare systems, as they focus more on saving money than on saving lives. That's why citizens experience long wait times, a lack of access to certain treatments, and substandard medical care.

Peter J. Pitts
New York

Sunday Dialogue: Equitable Healthcare

Originally published in *The New York Times*, March 25, 2012

To the Editor:

Starting on Monday, the Supreme Court will consider constitutional challenges to the Affordable Care Act, hearing arguments about Congressional authority to mandate the purchase of health insurance by individuals and threats to states' sovereignty by an expansion of state obligations under Medicaid.

Although not likely to be struck down in its entirety, the law will continue to face stubborn opposition accompanied by lingering charges that "death panels" will ration healthcare.

Many Americans mistakenly believe that Canada and Britain ration care while we do not. In reality, we also ration care, not through waiting lists but through high prices that impede access for those with no or limited insurance.

This inconvenient truth has been twisted into a convenient lie by reform opponents to confuse the public. The specter of rationing has also been invoked by those seeking to repeal the Independent Payment Advisory Board — a panel that would recommend ways to lower Medicare costs — so that Congress and special interests may retain firm control over Medicare spending cuts. By delegating responsibility to independent experts, such a board would help depoliticize the existing process.

Lost in the rhetoric is the Affordable Care Act's efforts to reduce rationing through mandatory coverage of preventive services and essential minimum benefits. The act holds promise for more rational allocation and consumption of scarce resources. But first, we must accept the fact that rationing already exists but needs to be made more equitable if we are to achieve better health for our citizens and better value for our healthcare dollars.

Alan B. Cohen
Boston, March 20, 2012

Readers React:

Professor Cohen criticizes those who want to repeal the Independent Payment Advisory Board for invoking "the specter of rationing." That ignores an immediate and crucial concern.

The board will be composed of 15 presidential appointees, unaccountable to the public. It will be given the task of cutting billions in Medicare expenditures — largely by denying government reimbursement for new and innovative medicines.

In other words, its only viable option will be to further ratchet down reimbursement rates for providers, especially doctors, who are already losing money on Medicare patients. Indeed, according to the American Medical Association, the financial burden of too-low payments under Medicare has driven 17 percent of doctors and 31 percent of primary care doctors out of the Medicare program altogether.

If rates fall any lower, seniors will have an increasingly difficult time securing doctor appointments. Visits will be cut short to squeeze in patients and care compromised. The board is even more insidious because it deflects policymakers' attention from innovative reform efforts with real cost-saving potential.

Peter J. Pitts
New York, March 21, 2012

Should We Suspend Patents on COVID Vaccines?

Originally published in *The New York Times*, July 5, 2021

To the Editor:

Re "The West Must Waive Drug Patents," by Walden Bello (Opinion guest essay, May 4):

Waiving vaccine patents will not result in swifter availability in less developed nations. Developing countries obviously need COVID-19 diagnostics, therapeutics, and vaccines as quickly as possible. But removing intellectual property protections could in fact slow that down.

In the past, when developing countries have issued "compulsory licenses" — which effectively allow domestic manufacturers to create knockoff treatments even before drug patents expire — it has taken years for generic manufacturers to receive the drug formulas and scale up production. Such extreme measures simply aren't necessary.

The companies that created lifesaving COVID-19 vaccines and therapies have already promised to share them widely in the developing world. Waiving patents wouldn't speed the rollout of existing vaccines, but it would ensure we're less prepared to fight the next pandemic, setting a terrible precedent that will chill future medical innovation.

Peter J. Pitts
New York

Making Sure the Drugs We Take Are Safe

Originally published in *The New York Times*, May 22, 2019

To the Editor:

Re "Can You Trust Generic Drugs?," by Katherine Eban (Sunday Review, May 12):

The answer is a qualified "yes," because guarantees of safety, effectiveness, and quality are only as sound as both regulator and manufacturer can ensure. When factory owners cheat on crucial quality measures (whether those facilities are in India, China, or the United States), all bets are off.

Absent robust quality control, therapeutic outcomes suffer and the public's trust in the Food and Drug Administration's (FDA) oversight of generic medicines wanes. Generic drugs help reduce costs, but the most expensive drug is the one that doesn't work.

The spread of subquality generic drugs must also serve as a warning as we enter into the era of biosimilars (FDA-approved copies of biologic medicines) that are also being manufactured around the world. FDA inspections must have a heavier global footprint, and that means an appropriate budget for overseas staffing.

Quality is by design and is nonnegotiable. As Aristotle reminds us, "Quality is not an act; it is a habit."

Peter J. Pitts
New York

What to Do About Drug Shortages?

Originally published in *The New York Times*, February 18, 2014

To the Editor:

Re "Drug Shortages Continue to Vex Doctors" (news article, February 11):

When it comes to addressing drug shortages, economic factors aren't just "a contributing factor"; they're the main factor.

Most of America's drug shortages arise in the generics market, where profitability is fairly low. This market can sustain only a handful of manufacturers, so when supply disruptions occur, there aren't a lot of additional producers (or in many cases any) in the market to pick up the slack.

Drugs that hold relatively stable prices, on the other hand, tend not to experience shortages, according to an October 2011 report by the Department of Health and Human Services. In other words, artificially low prices caused mainly by government programs — ranging from Medicaid to the problematic 340B discount drug program — have caused shortages. Where there's still a profit, there are rarely shortages.

Peter J. Pitts
Washington

Cost of Living: Who Gets New Drugs?

Originally published in *The New York Times*, December 8, 2008

To the Editor:

The National Institute for Health and Clinical Excellence in Britain is set to lift its ban on several kidney cancer drugs. The move will give patients access to lifesaving medicines that had previously been deemed "too costly" to cover under public health insurance.

This reversal is effectively an acknowledgment that the agency hasn't worked as intended. By denying patients access to cutting-edge treatments simply because of cost, it has heartlessly put lives at risk.

Peter J. Pitts
New York

Paths to Stopping Painkiller Overdoses

Originally published in *The New York Times*, April 25, 2014

To the Editor:

A report by the Institute of Medicine found that 100 million Americans are now living with chronic pain. That's a third of the country's population. Ten million of those have pain so severe that they are disabled by it. Pain costs the US economy $635 billion a year in lost productivity and healthcare expenses.

A vast majority of people who use opioids do so legally and safely. A subset uses these medications illegally. In fact, from 2010 to 2011, the number of Americans misusing and abusing opioid medications declined from 4.4 percent to 3.6 percent. In the debate over safe and effective pain medicines, context matters.

Peter J. Pitts
New York

Warnings Labels on Drugs

Originally published in *The New York Times*, June 11, 2011

To the Editor:

"Side Effects? These Drugs Have a Few" (Week in Review, June 5) rightly ridiculed the growing number of warning labels on prescription drugs. But it's the Food and Drug Administration's job to promote the safe and effective use of medications and medical technology.

Unfortunately, the current liability system encourages well-financed tort lawyers to view new product warnings or withdrawal decisions as signals to file lawsuits in hopes of securing a quick payday. Such irresponsible litigation doesn't make America's healthcare system safer — it just helps a small number of lawyers get rich.

Peter J. Pitts
New York

CONCLUDING THOUGHTS
Embracing Opportunity Management

"In giving advice, seek to help, not please, your friend." SOLON

The best way to positively impact the direction of the Next Normal is by being part of the solution. What does that mean? Firstly, it means recognizing that ecosystem problems require ecosystem solutions. There are few "eureka moments" generated by singular geniuses. The real formula is well known — blood, toil, tears, and sweat by dozens, hundreds, and thousands of dedicated healthcare professionals, patients, academicians, transnational organizations, and, yes — even politicians from every corner of the globe.

As the Japanese proverb goes, "Don't fix the blame, fix the problem." Moving forward successfully into the Next Normal calls for renewed focus not only on resource management and problem management but also on "opportunity management." We live in a time of boundless opportunity. We need to stay focused, stay positive, stay away from expedient solutions, and stay the course with science as our guide. The Next Normal is what we choose to make it. We are all in this together.

ABOUT THE AUTHOR

Peter Pitts is President of the Center for Medicine in the Public Interest. A former member of the United States Senior Executive Service, Pitts was FDA's Associate Commissioner for External Relations, serving as senior communications and policy adviser to the Commissioner.

His comments and commentaries on health care policy issues regularly appear in *The New York Times*, *The Chicago Tribune*, *The Washington Post*, and *The Wall Street Journal*, among others.

His book, *Become Strategic or Die*, is widely recognized as a cutting edge study of how leadership, in order to be successful over the long term, must be combined with strategic vision and ethical practice. He is the editor of *Coincidence or Crisis*, a discussion of global prescription medicine counterfeiting, *Physician Disempowerment: A Transatlantic Malaise*, and *Common Sense Healthcare Policy for Common Sense Americans (and Presidential Candidates)*.

He is a Visiting Professor at the University of Paris, Descartes Medical School, a Visiting Lecturer at the École Supérieure des Sciences Économiques et Commerciales (Paris and Singapore), and has served as an adjunct professor at Indiana University's School of Public and Environmental Affairs and Butler University. A graduate of McGill University, he is married to Jane Mogel, and has two sons.